JIMMY & ME

A Personal Memoir Of A Great Friendship:
JAMES DEAN & LEW BRACKER

By Lew Bracker

Copyright © 2013 Lewis Bracker All Rights Reserved

ISBN-10: 1940287014
ISBN-13: 978-1-940287-01-0

Cover photo credits: Gene Kornman/Warner Bros. 1955.

For My Daughters:

Alison and Lesley

Who Know Some of This Story —
but Not All of It.

ACKNOWLEDGEMENTS

Many people deserve my thanks. Here are a few of them.

Lee Raskin, historian and author, for his book *James Dean at Speed* (David Bull Publishing) which helped me with dates and races.

Hollis Evans, journalist and film producer out of USC who was a guide in the wilderness as she took me through the editing process and taught me quite a bit about how to write a book.

Leith Adams with Keith Burns for their book *James Dean: Behind the Scenes* (Carol Publishing Group). Their book with dates and events helped immensely with keeping my timeline straight.

Denise McCluggage for not taking no for an answer in urging me to write this book.

And finally, I want to thank my daughters for just being my daughters and for their valuable assistance while supporting me all the way through this experience.

FOREWORD

"I will never write a James Dean book."

I have said that many times over the years, and I was certain that I would not. I've had offers and many people urging me to do just that. I refused because I felt that my short but rich friendship with Jimmy Dean was personal and — as far as I was concerned — Jimmy and I continue to be the closest of friends for the last 57 years at this writing.

There have been over 200 books written about James Dean since his tragic death, with varying mixtures of fact and fantasy — rumors, innuendo, and simply false content. I didn't want to join the parade. Having written the book, I now know I actually avoided writing it because that meant opening a part of my mind to something I had locked away since 1955 — it meant revisiting a very important part of my life and examining my feelings.

You're now asking why I finally agreed to write this book. I will tell you. In October of 2011, I was an honoree in Monterey, California for a once-in-a-lifetime Porsche Race Car Classic where classic Porsches were going to be celebrated — including six from the Porsche Museum itself in Germany and many more from private collections — and as part of the festivities, I was one of a handful of former drivers "who made an important contribution to Porsche" between the years 1950-1965.

At a reception for invited guests only at Clint Eastwood's spectacular Tehama Golf Club, I met another honoree who had done her racing of Porsches on the East Coast. I had done mine primarily in California. Journalist Denise

McCluggage was starting a publishing company that would offer car books in digital form — eBooks. When the fact was revealed that James Dean had introduced me to Porsches and racing, Denise asked me, "Do you have a book?"

I told her of my resolve never to write one. She proceeded to try and change my mind, talking in terms of simply telling my own story of my friendship with James Dean, all the things that happened, all the things we did together, our conversations and feelings, and all of the events that we shared.

I would write a story — not about James Dean but about Jimmy Dean and Lew Bracker. I would write only what I knew. Nothing would be added. My younger daughter Lesley, who was with me in Monterey, urged me to do it — as did my daughter Alison when I told her about the idea.

Everyone who knows me well is aware of my excellent memory. In addition, I had written a lot of notes over the years concerning conversations Jimmy and I had, or events we experienced. You probably are asking yourself, "Why write notes if you weren't going to write a book?"

I did it so my daughters would have them. My girls have always wanted to know as much as possible about this very important period of my life. I did it for them to have and to hold this story, whether it gets published or not. But if you are reading this you know the outcome.

I have said this is not a book about James Dean, but a book about Jimmy Dean and Lew Bracker: a story about a very close friendship of 16 months that ended on Friday,

September 30, 1955. It is the story of a relationship between two young guys in 1950's Hollywood; two young men from very different backgrounds and with different pursuits; one still living at home with his parents and the other living on his own. One living within a strong traditional Jewish family structure (not Orthodox-cum-Kosher except when Grandma was visiting); the other lost his beloved mother at the age of nine and was sent on a train with his mother's body to his Aunt and Uncle, Ortense and Marcus Winslow, in Indiana. A nine-year-old with a familiar world suddenly gone and an upside down one thrust upon him.

It is the story of a great but short relationship. And I will put the rumors to rest right now — a very "straight" friendship. Different people have tried to determine why our friendship became so close, trying to see it through Jimmy's eyes. The late great film maker Robert Altman's first feature film, in conjunction with his then partner, writer/director George W. George, was Warner's *The James Dean Story* in which I appeared and did the driving of the Porsche Spyder. Bob had come to his own conclusions about our friendship. One early morning we were on our way to the fatal accident scene to film the re-enactment. We stopped in Castaic for breakfast and as we were waiting for our order, Bob turned to me and asked, "Why do you think Jimmy committed himself to the closest friendship he ever allowed himself to be a part of?" The question didn't surprise me. Bob was always trying to find out as much as possible about the mystery that was James Dean. I will always remember my answer clearly: "Jimmy knew he could trust me and was completely at ease and trusting in my company, around the house and with my family."

There are no rumors added to "spice" up the book and no scenarios or conversations invented. Nor have I inserted myself into situations where I was not personally involved. As the detective used to say on the old television show *Dragnet*, "Just the facts ma'am." But no names have been changed to protect the innocent.

I offer you then, the story of Jimmy and me — from my side of course, and with all my feelings, thoughts, takes, and hindsight wisdom — on the events and conversations of 57 years ago.

I now entrust them to you.

Lew Bracker
Palm Springs, California
April 30, 2013

"You were his rock — his center. You were straight-solid. You were the base that kept him centered when things were going crazy."

> **Robert Altman**
> Producer/Director
> *The James Dean Story*,
> Warner Brothers, 1956

Table of Contents

1.	In The Beginning	1
2.	We Did Lunch	7
3.	Babysitting And Guy Talk	11
4.	Pier	16
5.	The Beginning of a Beautiful Friendship	23
6.	A Place Called The Villa Capri	31
7.	Whispering In My Ear	41
8.	The "Dark" Movie	49
9.	A "Giant" Headache	57
10.	"Cisco"	64
11.	Two Guys And Two Porsches	72
12.	Summertime … And Stormy Weather	84
13.	"The Big Sneak"	96
14.	Off To The Races!	103
15.	And The Days Grow Short When You Reach September	115
16.	A World Of Hurt	124
17.	I Never Said Goodbye	133
18.	Epilogue	142
	About the Author	156
	About Fulcorte Press	157

Chapter One

IN THE BEGINNING

I have always been of the opinion that things happen because they are meant to. If you look back on life or history itself, you will find that certain things had to happen at the exact moment they did for the event in question to have taken place at all. Most of the times these moments pass without any notice as to their importance, or that they may lead to a more significant event in our future. And in some cases our immediate future.

I was born in Nogales, Arizona: a border town on the Mexican border in the Southern Arizona Mountains, a town of about 5,000 people in what was once Apache territory of the Apache Nation of Cochise and Geronimo. Many of my aunts and uncles (some ten sets of them and about 35 cousins) also lived in Nogales and in most instances just across the street or a block away; and all went to the same small schools. We were a very close family, both emotionally and geographically.

I always pictured our family structure as a large temple-like ceiling held up by strong pillars. Those pillars were my aunts and uncles whose closeness made all of us cousins close. Since the cousins were in and out of each other's homes all the time, the cousins were more like siblings. I had so many first and second-cousins in Nogales that when I was kindergarten age, I thought every kid in my school was either a Mexican-American or a cousin.

My parents made a big decision in 1939 that changed my life completely as well as that of my older brother Howard and my sister Midge. We moved from Nogales to Los Angeles. We went directly from our summer at the beach to a home in L.A. This was a very bold and emotional step to take within our family, but my dad always thought outside the box and he wanted us to go to better schools. My parents placed great importance on education and it was actually a better location for his growing business. A few years later, after finishing high school, my cousin Adele Bracker, who was the daughter of my dad's brother Charlie and a peer of my older sister Midge, came to live with us in L.A. for a year in order to attend Business College. This is how the family interacted and it helps make my point that if the family hadn't been this close, Jimmy and I would never have met.

Adele was a pianist and enrolled at the University of California, Berkeley, in the late 1940's studying music. It was here she met a young composer from Brooklyn, N.Y., Leonard Rosenman. Lenny had come out to study composition under the famed modern composer and teacher, Roger Sessions. Adele and Lenny met and they married.

This turned out to be the first event in the chain that, at the time, seemed to have no impact on my life. My dad had purchased El Capitan Ranch in 1946; seventeen miles north of Santa Barbara, with two and a half miles of beach front. My folks put a war surplus army house on beach "point" and contracted to have the house renovated and a large covered front porch added. Dad also allowed his brother Charlie, Adele's father, to do the same. As a result, I met Lenny Rosenman in the summer of 1947, when he and Adele came down to the ranch on their honeymoon to stay for a week in her father's beach house. I was the only one at the beach houses because I had been handed the job of painting our house, and the family wasn't coming up until later in the summer when it would be finished. This is how I first met Lenny, and was even a part of his honeymoon.

Jimmy & Me

Lenny and I became great friends. In 1950, I was in the Army courtesy of the North Koreans and stationed at Ft. Ord, California, just a few miles from Monterey and Carmel. On some weekends I used to drive up to Berkeley and spend the weekend with Adele, Lenny and their brand new daughter, Danielle. I later visited Adele and Lenny in the N.Y. apartment they had moved to after leaving the University of California.

I see this as the period when Lenny and I crossed over from being family by marriage to a lasting friendship. I used to talk music with Lenny and we used to laugh a lot when we were together, particularly about the family.

While living in N.Y., Adele and Lenny were invited to a party at a friend's apartment — a normal happening in N.Y. Lenny was a great conversationalist and enjoyed expounding on many topics. He loved to talk! One of the reasons we became good friends is because I loved to listen. As time proved, Lenny was a very talented composer, and he could mesmerize you talking about music. Being an accomplished pianist, Lenny also played at parties if the feeling moved him, and at this particular party Lenny impressed a young Broadway actor who was in attendance.

As Lenny told me, "I was standing there, and this young actor came over and introduced himself as Jimmy Dean. He then immediately began asking a lot of questions about music and composers. Several hours later Adele and I went home and I didn't think about Jimmy again. However, a few nights later the doorbell rang. I opened the door and there was Jimmy. He immediately said, 'I want you to teach me music.'" One of Jimmy's most apparent characteristics was his intense curiosity, not just about the world in general, but about each individual he met along the way. Jimmy was the consummate "brain picker."

Lew Bracker

Lenny had coffee with Jimmy a few times, got friendly, and actually began to teach Jimmy the basic rudiments of composition and music theory. But eventually Jimmy lost patience because it was taking too long. The lessons stopped, but Jimmy and Lenny became close friends. In fact, it was Jimmy who urged the director Elia Kazan to hire this unknown composer to supply the music for Jimmy's first film, *East of Eden*.

Lenny, talking to me about Jimmy, once said, "He likes to deal in headlines," meaning that Jimmy just wanted to learn a little about everything, whether it was music, bullfighting, bongos, dancing, or roping, so that he could talk about them. I didn't and don't agree. Jimmy was curious about everything and wanted to learn. But he was impatient — except for his craft. Jimmy had infinite patience in learning his craft. Jimmy knew that he would be learning his craft forever. But having said that, I did observe in Jimmy that there were some things he wanted to sample, but once sampled, he lost interest. Speaking with his cousin Marcus, I brought this up, and Marcus said, "Yes, I can remember things like that. One day he decided he wanted to paint the basement and when he was half done, he lost interest and just left it.' My take on this is that Jimmy wanted to experience painting a wall or something, and half way through, he satisfied his curiosity. The basement remained half-painted for years.

After Lenny was signed to compose the score for *East of Eden*, the family, which now included two daughters, moved back to California in early April 1954. At that time there was a two-story building, long and narrow, just across the street from the Warner Bros. studios. The first floor housed a drug store, and the second floor comprised apartments, usually occupied by unknown actors working at Warner. The Rosenmans and their two young daughters, Danielle and Gabrielle, were lucky enough to get the end apartment, which was a two-bedroom

Jimmy & Me

with a large oval living room/dining room. Next door in a studio apartment lived the actress Lois Smith, also making her film debut in *Eden*. And next to her was Richard Davalos, who played Jimmy's brother Aron in the movie, doing the same. The apartment's proximity to both Lois Smith's and Dick Davalos' apartments was instrumental in my meeting and knowing both of them, and becoming friends with Dick Davalos, a very good young actor from Broadway and a very nice guy.

One Saturday in early June, 1954, I was hanging around the house listening to music on my hi-fi (so-called at that time). I have always loved music — classical, jazz, Big Band and Broadway. Being knowledgeable about music and music history (I played the trumpet since school), I was in awe of Lenny's talent. The phone rang and it was Lenny. "It's me Lenny; we're back in L.A. I'm a big Hollywood composer, so come on over to Warners for lunch," he laughed. "That's what they do in this town." He invited me to come over and have lunch with him in the Green Room, the cafe on the Warner lot. I told him, "I've always wanted to do lunch, but my people have to call your people. However, just name the day." I was happy to accept the invite, not because it was lunch on a movie lot — growing up in L.A. I had done that before — but because being reunited with Lenny was a pleasure. We made a date for the following week.

I grew up with Hollywood all around me but I was never interested in being in the "business." If I had been, my dad knew some important people who were friends who could and would have got me started. In 1954 I had been out of the Army for only eight months, and back in the United States for the same length of time. I was enjoying civilian life again, reveling in it really, and I wasn't thinking too deeply about anything — including my future. I was definitely in the present. I knew I wanted to be a "big businessman," but I didn't know what kind of business I wanted to be involved with. So I tried insurance first. It was as casual as that. I did know one thing though — I did not want to work for someone else.

Jimmy and I were starting our journey from the opposite shores of a great ocean of different childhood and teen experiences. Jimmy was working on his first film, knew exactly where he wanted to go, and was totally focused on his craft and his future.

One could say that the differences in our life experiences were as vast as the difference between a venetian blind and a blind Venetian. We were so different we were somehow the same.

Chapter Two

WE DID LUNCH

It was a day like most San Fernando Valley summer days, sunny and bright — and at that time those days were as clear as the proverbial bell. The main item on my agenda that day was lunch with Lenny Rosenman at Warner Brothers Studios. Lenny and Adele were really enjoying the studio scene, meeting interesting people and going to parties. Lenny in particular totally embraced the role of a new composer from N.Y. with a "genius" label attached — courtesy of James Dean, his "advance man" on the lot. I was anticipating seeing Lenny and the Green Room with all of the hustle, bustle, intrigues, and familiar screen faces that went with the experience. I found the Green Room, entered and looked around for Lenny. I spotted him and walked over to the booth. I remember that the booth was on the right two booths down from the doorway as you entered the main room. (There was also a private room where Jack Warner and his minions dined when in the Green Room).

I hadn't seen Lenny since I visited N.Y. He and Adele had been busy getting themselves settled into the apartment. So he got up as I approached and we embraced in the traditional Mexican way — an "embracio", which we had both adopted from the way of life in Nogales, and which has now become a popular way of male friends greeting each other. There was another guy with Lenny whom he introduced to me as Jimmy Dean, and I recall that Lenny's and my happy greeting was not lost on Jimmy. I said "Hi," and shook hands with Jimmy, who sat across from Lenny and me, but I only knew Jimmy at that moment as a friend of Lenny — or at least someone he met on the Warner lot. I was not privy to their relationship in New York at that time, and was more interested in catching up with Lenny. Jimmy simply stuck out his hand to shake, sizing me up more than shaking hands. Lenny and I proceeded to talk, reminisce, and laugh throughout the entire lunch, particularly about his father-in-law, my Uncle Charlie, who was a favorite target of our humor. When Adele brought Lenny home to my strait-laced uncle, it was as if she'd brought back an alien! For instance, Lenny wore a corduroy suit that prompted my uncle to exclaim he was dressed for a vaudeville act. Throughout the lunch, Jimmy slouched in a corner of the booth where it meets the wall — one leg stretched out taking up the rest of the bench space. As I got to know him better, I realized this was the sign of Jimmy relaxing and trusting.

Jimmy didn't add much during the early part of our lunch as we laughed about family things, but he was very interested in the interaction between Lenny and me. Jimmy had a great respect for Lenny's mind, and that made him interested in anyone Lenny clearly enjoyed and respected. Jimmy watched and listened intently. Not knowing Jimmy at the time, I couldn't realize that Jimmy was slowly letting down his guard.

When Lenny got around to giving me a little background on Jimmy — telling me that he was one of the stars in *East of Eden*; they knew each other in New York, and had come out to Hollywood together for the film — Jimmy got more involved in the conversation with his own cryptic remarks about Hollywood, the Green Room protocol, and some of his fellow cast members. I asked why they called it "The Green Room," and Jimmy shot back, "because everyone in here is jealous of somebody else." Gradually, he joined our convivial conversation. I remember, in particular, Lenny and I were laughing and joking about how Jack Warner had a private dining room and would invite (order) his contract producers to lunch

Jimmy & Me

with him, and how these high-salaried and famous screen names were afraid to say "no" and became luncheon sycophants. Jimmy joined in with "and it's like musical chairs. They fight over the chair on Jack's right and on his left." I asked "what do they talk about in there?" Jimmy, getting into it now, replied, "probably how to get me out of my dressing room." Lenny, prodding Jimmy, asked "what would you do if Jack invited you to one of his lunches?" Jimmy never hesitated: "I'd go right in there, sit next to Jack Warner, take my teeth out, put them right in front of him, and say let's eat!" We all laughed.

Early in our lunch, an interesting scene played out in front of me, providing me with important insights into the inter-relationships between some actors. I caught a glimpse of the competition that exists between actors. As we were waiting for our lunch orders, Paul Newman came into the cafe. Paul had also come from Broadway, was signed by Warner Bros., and had also tested for the part of Cal in *East of Ede*n – the part that Jimmy got. Paul not only didn't get this role, but was cast in a typical 1950's Technicolor "epic," *The Silver Chalice* — a highly forgettable film. Worse yet, Paul was garbed in full Roman regalia — skirt, armor, all of it. He was clearly embarrassed that day standing at the table in front of us, a serious Broadway actor from the Actor's Studio who had been brought to Hollywood only to be dumped into a religious potboiler in a role that any Hollywood hack could mail in.

Paul seemed to be a personable and friendly guy, and he came over to exchange pleasantries. Jimmy seemed a little condescending, and produced that kind of half-smile/half-smirk that I was to become so accustomed to seeing. Jimmy said, "You win some, you lose some, but you do look cute in that dress." This may sound mean, but Jimmy was revealing a New York serious actor's view of Hollywood, and meant it sardonically. Paul Newman was clearly out of sorts regarding his current lot.

Lew Bracker

Jimmy acted like he had the higher ground, having won the role of Cal in *Eden* over Paul. I must say that the three of them — Lenny, Jimmy and Paul — treated Paul's misfortune, in the short term, with light humor. I always remembered that meeting, and the irony that it was later touched with: after Jimmy's death, Paul inherited at least two major film roles that Jimmy was meant to do — *The Left Handed Gun*, and *Somebody up There Likes Me*.

When lunch was finished and we walked outside, Nick Dennis, a character actor on *Eden*, jumped on Jimmy, throwing his arms around him with a big smile and laugh on his face. I was to learn that Nick was very much like the characters he played on the screen, a devil-may-care Greek running rampant. Jimmy obviously enjoyed Nick. We hung around outside for a few minutes, Lenny, Jimmy, Nick and me — just kibitzing, and then went our separate ways. I enjoyed the lunch even more than I had anticipated.

Driving home after the lunch, which in traffic-free 1954 took only ten minutes, I mulled the lunch over in my mind, like revisiting a pleasant memory. I was aware on some level of liking Jimmy and finding him very interesting, and thought that I might run into him again, maybe at Lenny and Adele's. But having gone our separate ways after lunch, it all could have just as easily ended there. We had shared a lunch with Lenny, dominated by Lenny; there were no sparks, no rockets shooting off and, at least on my part, no sense of thinking or planning that we would meet again unless through our common friend, Lenny Rosenman. James Dean was just another guy at the lunch table, until Lenny told me he was in *East of Eden*. Even then, I assumed he was simply a featured player. No one had mentioned anything about co-starring. And as far as the movie-going public was concerned, he was unknown.

Chapter Three

BABYSITTING AND GUY TALK

A week or so after that lunch, I got a phone call from Adele saying that she and Lenny had received a VIP invitation from Warner to the première of one of their new big films. Adele really wanted to go — they were having a ball doing the Hollywood thing — but couldn't find a babysitter. Would I come over and sit for their girls? "Sure." At that time there was no cable or satellite TV. L.A. had seven over-the-air TV stations, and at least three of those had a movie every night. I had nothing on for the night, and I could watch a TV movie at their apartment as easily as at home.

That particular night found me sitting on the couch in the Rosenman apartment watching "*The Million Dollar Movie*" or whatever. The girls were already asleep by 9:00 p.m. It was a warm night, so the front door, leading to the narrow outside main hallway, stood wide open. In those days you didn't worry about doors being unlocked.

I was slouched on the couch watching an old film (the only kind they showed then) when a man filled the open doorway. The hall was dark so I couldn't make out who it was at first. Then I realized it was James Dean.

Jimmy gave me a casual, "Hi; what are you doing here?" while still standing in the doorway. "Watching a flick and sitting the girls," I replied, and explained where Lenny and Adele were. Jimmy made no comment; he just came in and sat down in one of two upholstered chairs opposite the couch. He flopped one leg over the arm of the chair and glanced at the TV. Jimmy did not live in the apartment building anymore, although many Warner contract actors did live in that building. Instead, he was living (illegally) in his dressing room, really an apartment, on the Warner lot during the *East of Eden* shooting, so he just walked over from there. This was something he did quite often, as Adele was a good Jewish homemaker, and he knew that he could always eat with the Rosenmans when the mood took him.

When Jimmy appeared in the doorway, I was aware of feeling pleased but not surprised. I somehow knew after our lunch that I was going to see him again and get to know him better. I also felt, instinctively, that he was not an ordinary person. I had no idea that Jimmy would become a big Hollywood star, and certainly not in his first film. And really, I didn't care about that. Jimmy sent electricity into any room he entered. I just wanted to talk to him some more to get to know him.

And talk we did. We kind of half-watched the movie, but Jimmy began to converse by asking me a few questions about myself. Jimmy asked, "What do you do? Lenny said something about insurance." I told Jimmy about having just returned from the Army, and explained that I was working for a friend of my dad for the time being. Jimmy followed by asking, "Is that what you want to do?" And I told him, "I haven't the faintest, but I'll find my niche." Jimmy continued with questions about where I live, and I responded that I lived at home, which was not out of the ordinary in the '50's. Jimmy clearly had no interest in watching the movie, but he wasn't leaving, either.

Jimmy had an intense curiosity and he was a world-class brain picker, but he seemed to have a personal interest in me. I hardly asked him any questions because I was so busy answering his. I replied to all of his questions about my life up until that time, and eventually blurted out that I was "carrying a torch" for a

Jimmy & Me

girl, a term used in those days to describe a lost romance. I also revealed, surprising even myself, that this was the first girl I ever asked to marry me.

I still can't believe I confided in Jimmy, because I am a very private person about my personal business. But Jimmy absolutely zeroed in on what I was telling him: "We had something special from the first chance meeting, and we saw each other every day after that. And one night I asked her to marry me, and she didn't hesitate, she just said that she didn't feel that way about me. I sunk right into the ground. I thought surely she was going to say yes." I hadn't a clue, but I had just pushed Jimmy's button. He wanted to know all about it. "How, when did you meet her?" he asked, and when I answered, he followed immediately with, "How often did you see each other" and "Did you meet her folks; did she meet yours?" He wanted all the details, and then wanted to know, "What made you so sure she was going to say yes?" "I don't know; I just felt it. We started seeing each other immediately after meeting at a pool party."

Jimmy paused, seemingly digesting all of this information, but then he began to tell me about his troubles with his current girlfriend. I learned later that it was quite a leap for Jimmy to open up about his private life. He began by saying, "I am really serious about this girl, but I don't want to get married yet. She's an actress; in fact she's making a film at Warners right now." I have always been a very good listener, and I just sat there letting Jimmy talk. "We met on the lot, and have been seeing each other ever since." He then revealed, "Her name is Pier. Pier Angeli." I knew who she was, because I had seen her on the movie screen. I remembered her as slim, delicate and very pretty. I had never met her, nor did I ever.

Lew Bracker

I remember my response: "She's very pretty." I really didn't think that this conversation would go any further, but Jimmy continued. "Pier is not refusing me; in fact she wants to get married, now. The problem is her mother hates me." Only then did I realize that Jimmy needed to talk about this to someone, and that he had decided on me. He went on to explain, "Her mother is very Catholic, and only a Catholic Italian or Italian-American can marry Pier. I'm everything she does not want in a son-in-law." Jimmy paused, so I said, "Wow; that's pretty heavy."

"Atlas had a lighter load," Jimmy replied with that half grin of his. So, we kind of sat there and consoled each other, but my situation was over and Jimmy was, at least on the outside, optimistic about his.

Jimmy really took me by surprise with his next revelation, not so much by what he told me, but that he told me at all. "Right now," he said, "we've got to be very careful. Her mother suspects Pier is seeing me, but doesn't know for sure, so we meet secretly at night in my dressing room, where no one can spy on us." Jimmy was really divulging personal information, yet he hardly knew me! "Her mother is like the Great Wall of China between us," he added, " we have to meet in secret, love in secret, and even write in secret — all because I am not Italian or Catholic." I do know, and have always known, that we first bonded that night when the conversation turned to our romantic problems. One thing is certain, once we got on this subject, we really warmed towards each other. Before we knew it, the movie that we hadn't paid any attention to was now over — and so was the evening. Our mutual love for Porsches and racing was only uncovered later on.

Jimmy announced he was leaving, but remained standing in the doorway. He kind of dawdled, awkwardly hanging around.

Jimmy & Me

Leaving but not leaving. "I'll probably be seeing you around," he mumbled, "with Lenny or something. Adele and Lenny will be coming back soon, so I'll see you later." I had the feeling that Jimmy wanted to prolong the evening, but not with Lenny and Adele there. He appeared to be debating inwardly about whether or not to suggest meeting up at a later date. But he finally left, saying only, "See ya." Jimmy's departure was just as casual as his arrival.

After Jimmy left, I checked on the girls, who I had almost forgotten were there. I found them sleeping soundly and totally unaware of what turned out to be a very important event in my young life.

Chapter Four

PIER

Jimmy and Pier had, by early August 1954, both finished shooting their films on the Warner lot, so Pier was no longer at Warner Bros. Gone was the convenience of getting together in Jimmy's apartment-like dressing room, something they did often. It was now quite difficult for them to meet — either clandestinely or accidentally on purpose — at the studio. Yet Jimmy was seeing as much as possible of Pier. He still had his Warner dressing room, and didn't give that up until the end of the year or thereabouts.

One night, during this time period, I came home from seeing a movie at about 10:00. My mother was up, and she greeted me with, "You missed Jimmy by about a half-hour. He drove up and had a girl with him, and called out to see if you were home." I asked if she knew who the girl was (I went right to the interesting part), and my mother said she didn't know; she looked slim and had dark hair under a bandanna. I learned later it was Pier. Jimmy was bringing her by to meet me ... something I was never to do.

Pier's mother was ever the obstructionist, and now that her daughter was no longer at Warner Bros. and basically back at home, she was able to exert more stringent control. She was always in Pier's ear about Jimmy in a very negative way. More importantly, she did a good job of controlling who Pier could and could not see, and even who she could and could not talk to. She even intercepted Pier's phone calls and mail. James Dean was at the top of her mother's "could not" list.

Jimmy & Me

By now, Jimmy trusted me more and more, and began talking to me about his heart-breaking situation. He knew that he could tell me his innermost feelings, and that they would never go any further than my ears. This was very much a case of a young guy in love pouring out his heart to his closest friend. "Pier wants to defy her mother and run off and marry me, but I don't want to get married yet. I want to marry Pier, but I have too much to do first," Jimmy told me. "We have time." He then added, "Pier is scared. She is sure that if we wait, her mother will somehow squash this whole thing." Ever the listener, I offered only support. I don't know which is the greater pain: unrequited love, as I had experienced at the time I met Jimmy, or a love that could never be — a star-crossed love.

One evening we were standing out in front of my parents' house. The house sat back some 20 yards and half-way up a hill overlooking Studio City and the San Fernando Valley. The twenty yards were asphalted parking and turn around space, and bordered by a knee-high log fence. We were standing out there looking out over the Valley, talking about Pier's mother and how she constantly opened Pier's mail — in case Jimmy sent a letter to the house — when he suddenly said, "I'm going to be able to get you a lot of insurance business. You know, Pier and her friends have a lot of jewelry and stuff that has to be insured, and they'll all insure through you."

I felt a little embarrassed by this because it was not in my nature to approach any friend or family seeking business, but I understood that Jimmy was thinking of doing something for me — and he also was including me in his and Pier's future.

Later on, when we both owned Porsches, we were up on Mulholland Drive one night, parked at a dirt off-road spot (and those spots are still there) looking at the San Fernando Valley's floor of lights and just mixing silence with casual talk as good friends will do. Jimmy said to me, "Lew, you have the gift of objectivity." "Oh?" I answered. Jimmy went on to say, "Yeah, you see things, the whole picture for what it is." Jimmy was silent for a few seconds as I was, because I didn't know what to say or where this was going. And then Jimmy asked me, "What's your gut feeling? Do you think it will work out the way I think it will?" Jimmy was looking right at me and not at the view. He was looking at me and I knew exactly what Jimmy was talking about, he was talking about his relationship with Pier.

I also knew that Jimmy had an optimistic view of his romance with Pier. I was being asked for total honesty, and I was going to respond in-kind and Jimmy knew it. Using a phrase for the first time in my memory, but one I would use a few times through my life, I said: "This isn't going to end well — I hope to God it does — but unless Pier gets herself out of her mother's clutches, she is her mother's pawn." I don't think I surprised Jimmy with my answer. I know that deep down Jimmy felt this was a battle he was going to lose. I tried to soften my answer by saying: "Jimmy, if you spend your life trying to please everyone else or even just someone, you'll never have a life of your own, and that's what is going on with Pier. She might please her mother but she'll never have a life of her own and she is going to be very unhappy."

Right up until that night, Jimmy never gave an outward sign that he thought Pier's mother would be able to break them up, that he would ever lose Pier. He thought their secret trysts would eventually become a public romance, which it did, and that the momentum would overpower Pier's mother's objections. The only reason Jimmy hung on to living in his dressing room apartment at Warner was so that he and Pier had a place where Pier's mother had no control. But when Jimmy began that conversation on the subject atop Mulholland, I, for the first time, thought that not only did Jimmy doubt living "happily ever

Jimmy & Me

after" with Pier, but knew it would never happen, and looked to me for confirmation. We were young then, really just kids, and I have since learned that there is no "happily ever after," there is just life — and everything in life is temporary.

Jimmy never sat down to tell me the "Pier story" from start to finish, but would feed me bits and pieces when things were bad: "Her mother is causing a lot of trouble," he said once, and "she has Pier crying all the time." And then: "She won't let Pier take a phone call from me." Or: "She wants a Catholic son-in-law." Still, early on, Jimmy kept telling himself that things would work themselves out in the end and until that time, they would manage to meet and romance. That night on Mulholland was, in my view, Jimmy hitting the wall — coming to grips with reality — and I had never seen him so vulnerable.

The dam burst in October 1954 with the sudden announcement that Pier was marrying Vic Damone. I had no idea where Vic Damone came from. His name was never mentioned in our conversations and, as far as I knew, neither he nor anyone else was in the picture. Pier did meet Vic Damone some three years before, I later learned, but that meeting didn't appear to register at all with Pier. Pier's mother was not in the equation at that time, but she was now in full battle mode.

Damone was the perfect son-in-law for Pier's mother: Catholic, of Italian descent, and non-controversial. It was something that Pier's mother had to make happen, and she did. It was a short engagement, more like a shotgun wedding. I wonder if the mother's desperation was fueled by the fact that, after *Giant*, Jimmy was due to star in *Somebody up There Likes Me* with Pier as the female lead. I can't say, because I don't know if *Somebody up There* was even in the conversation at that time, but it brings up a plethora of interesting questions: if Jimmy had not been killed, would Pier's role have gone to some other actress? If it had not gone to another actress, would Jimmy and Pier have resumed their romance even though Pier was now married? What would have been Jimmy's attitude, or Pier's for that matter? We will never know, and I won't speculate. But just think about it — Jimmy and Pier not only on the same lot, but working on the same set. Don't forget, Jimmy and Pier didn't formally split up, although you may have read otherwise. Pier's mother engineered it all.

Jimmy disappeared for a few days over the time of the wedding day. I later learned from Jimmy that he just wanted to be alone and that he had got on his motorcycle, against studio orders, driven to the church, and just sat out there while Pier was being married. I didn't ask him about it at all — Jimmy told me what he wanted to tell me. A few days later, Jimmy and I picked up the strings of our friendship. After Jimmy came back from *Giant*'s Marfa, Texas location, we never discussed Pier again. I don't say Jimmy never thought of her. He was seeing Ursula by then, but there were times when Jimmy was quieter, introspective. That was the only outward sign he gave, but I knew he was hurting inside. Jimmy was an actor — a great actor — and to me he was hiding a deep wound.

We resumed our meandering around town, and usually ended up at our favorite haunt, the Villa Capri. But one night, at about 10:00 p.m., Jimmy said, "Let's drive out to the beach." I said I knew of a place called Castle Rock in between Santa Monica and Malibu. The rock sat just off the Pacific Coast Highway, and most times you could climb right onto it with the tide just licking at the foot of the Rock. That really suited Jimmy's mood, so that is where we went. We parked and climbed onto Castle Rock. We probably spent about three hours out there, mostly just listening to the waves and looking at a sky full of stars with an occasional shooting star to make a wish on, if so inclined. It was a night where we were lost in our own thoughts. I never

Jimmy & Me

asked Jimmy what was on his mind, but that night I felt that Jimmy was thinking of Pier.

About a year later, one evening in August 1955 around 10:00 p.m., Jimmy and I were sitting in the Villa Capri. We had finished eating, and were just sitting there talking when Vic Damone, Pier Angeli's husband, entered the restaurant. After a few minutes at the bar, he came over to our table carrying a bottle of champagne and three glasses. He smiled and said hello. I had no idea what was coming or how Jimmy was going to act, but I felt decidedly uncomfortable. I also felt every eye in the Villa on us. Vic said, "I would be honored if you will help me celebrate. Tonight I am a father!" I was at once looking for a hole to crawl into, and trying to look at both Vic Damone and Jimmy. I was trying to figure out if Vic was being vicious or gracious. I couldn't even imagine how Jimmy was going to react. I did not want to be there.

Jimmy seemed relaxed, slouching in a corner of the booth as he usually did, and with his half-smile (smirk?) said words I will never forget: "That's one baby I will definitely drink to."

I did not then, or ever, ask Jimmy exactly what he was intimating — but I drew my own conclusions at the time — and everyone else can draw theirs. We did toast the newborn child with Vic Damone's champagne. A few light pleasantries were exchanged, and Vic moved on.

Jimmy and I stayed there and conversed as if the little scene had never taken place. I realized after Vic left that for all that time he had been there, I had been waiting to exhale. Jimmy didn't mention the incident ever again, so neither did I. I never again heard any mention made of Vic Damone, Pier Angeli, or the baby from Jimmy.

Lew Bracker

In thinking about that night: I find it significant that in the short conversation and toast, no mention was made of Pier by either Vic or Jimmy. But Pier's presence in that booth was overwhelming. Even though Pier gave birth by Caesarian section, a fact I did not know at the time and I am sure Jimmy didn't either, Vic didn't mention anything about her well-being.

Chapter Five

THE BEGINNING OF
A BEAUTIFUL FRIENDSHIP

In early June of 1954, the phone rang at home and I picked it up. It was Jimmy. There was no preamble or explanation about having been on location, just a "come over to the studios and have lunch." And he meant *that day*. This was the first time Jimmy ever called me. I never knew how he got my home phone, but I assume he got it from Lenny. At that time, I didn't have his number. Jimmy and I were to hardly ever talk on the phone. Our conversations were short, restricted to where and when we were meeting, but even that was rare, because Jimmy would usually drop by without notice. I did the same, although I did call Jimmy one day to tell him about the new Spyder in Competition Motors' window. The longest conversation we ever had on the phone was our last conversation on September 30, 1955.

For the first time since our night in the Rosenman apartment, Jimmy and I were meeting again in the Green Room. I wasn't aware of it at the time, but Jimmy's choice of venue was his way of publicly declaring our friendship, as opposed to meeting for a drink or a cup of coffee at the Hamburger Hamlet. Of significance, of course, was the fact that Jimmy set up this meeting, wanted this meeting, wanted to see me again. That was not lost on me.

At the restaurant, Jimmy and I met like old friends. He seemed to be in a good mood, so I assumed the filming was going well and we talked about the usual things — women and cars. I had a love of cars, but I had no interest in foreign sports cars at that time. Sports cars in the early fifties consisted of MG's, Jaguars, and myriad cheaper British underpowered machines, but at the top in the sports car world were the Germans: Mercedes-Benz, and the smaller but amazing Porsches. Jimmy seemed to be on a mission to convert me. "The Benz team with Fangio (Juan Manuel of Argentina) and Moss (Stirling of England) are dominating the European Circuit," he said. He was talking cars even before girls and romance. I wasn't at all familiar with what he was talking about, but I was very interested. I had seen the gull-winged Benz on the road in L.A. and loved it as a car. "What about Ferrari?" I asked. I did know about Ferrari. "Benz is beating them at Le Mans, Nürburgring, Mille Miglia; you name it," Jimmy answered.

Jimmy had bought a red 1953 MG-TD in May. In fact, after lunch, Jimmy showed me the car and said, "Hop in! We'll go back to the sound stage." So off we went. I have to tell you that the MG-TD made a lot of noise and sounded like it was really ripping down the road, when in fact, it was slow. And when you consider that the noise is compounded by the fact that the studio lot streets go between the sound stages and the sound just keeps bouncing off the buildings, you get an idea of what Jimmy was really doing. Jimmy asked, "How do you like it?" and I answered, "It makes a lot of noise, but it doesn't go anywhere!" Jimmy really got a laugh out of that.

"I bought this because Jack Warner won't let me ride my bike (motorcycle) or be on anyone else's bike until the end of my contract," he explained. This was half of the drama being played out between Jimmy and Jack Warner. The other half was Jimmy living on the lot in his dressing room. By roaring up and down the studio streets, Jimmy was thumbing his nose at Jack Warner. We ended up at the sound stage where *Eden* was filming interior scenes.

Jimmy & Me

This was my first visit onto the set of *Eden* and my first glimpse into the undercurrents, the interactions between Jimmy and some of the cast. For some reason, Jimmy didn't care for his co-star in Eden, Dick Davalos. Jimmy, in my opinion, had a condescending attitude towards Dick. To me, he was a very nice guy who was very enthusiastic about life and set on enjoying it. It turned out that during the time Jimmy was out of town for the now-famous *Life Magazine* shoot and some New York live TV dramas, I spent some time with Dick Davalos. He didn't have a car so I took him up to our ranch for a day, a trip he loved, and one night we went down to the beach. In all three of his films, though, Jimmy never introduced me to principal actors on any of his pictures. The sole exceptions, besides Davalos, were Liz Taylor on *Giant* and Burl Ives on *Eden*. He did make a point of introducing me to stunt people, grips, character actors, and camera people, however. These were the people that really interested Jimmy — these were the brains he could pick. Actors didn't interest him.

He did not introduce me to a Raymond Massey or Rock Hudson, but made a point of having me meet Nick Dennis, a supporting actor. As for Mr. Massey, Jimmy didn't respect him at all as an actor, thinking he was too stiff and too wooden (he had the same problem with Rock Hudson). Once, when talking to me about Raymond Massey, he quipped, "It's like working with the Frankenstein Monster." Elia Kazan advised Jimmy to use that in his role in *Eden*, because that was just the dynamic he wanted between Cal and his father. If you watch *Eden* again you will see how apparently cold and wooden Massey is to Jimmy's search for love and approval. Jimmy's opinion? "Perfect casting," he told me.

One week later, Jimmy, who now had my office number, called and invited me to lunch with him at the studio again. I don't know if Jimmy specifically wanted me to meet the actor who

Lew Bracker

was joining us, or if it just happened, but to my great pleasure we were joined by Burl Ives. Burl was famous as "America's Troubadour" long before he was in films, and before coffee houses and guitar singer/players of folk music hit the big time in the 60's. He was a fun-loving and very interesting man.

As a music lover, I was very aware of Burl Ives. When I was a teen and the *Saturday Evening Post* was the most popular magazine in America, they did a feature article on Burl Ives that I remember reading. Also, I loved to listen to him sing on the radio. Burl had his own CBS show in the 1940's. He also sang on radio stations across the country as he traveled the byways of our country. Burl was 46 at this time and was already known as a singer, actor and recording artist. Americans loved when he sang of Americana in folk songs such as "Ghost Riders In The Sky," "Foggy, Foggy Dew," "The Blue Tail Fly (Jimmy Crack Corn)," and "Lavender Blue."

After lunch, Jimmy went back for some shooting, but Burl was free and had told us about his car, an early 1930s Packard limo with a separate driver's compartment, and a passenger compartment separated from the driver by a roll-up window. As one who loves classic cars, I oohed and aahed over the machine. Burl insisted on taking me for a ride, and also insisted on my sitting in the back while he played chauffeur. As it turned out, it was a short ride. We were partway up the hill that would take us back to Ventura Boulevard when Burl pulled in to what was, and still is a Burbank landmark: The Smokehouse Restaurant.

Burl loved to talk and he had plenty of stories to tell. He spoke about his life of traveling around the country singing songs like "Cool Clear Water," "Big Rock Candy Mountain," and "On Top Of Old Smokey". "Ya know, I was arrested once for singing "Foggy, Foggy Dew," Burl told me. "The locals thought it was "bawdy" so they arrested me on vagrancy. My middle name is

Jimmy & Me

Ivanhoe," he confessed. "Nobody really knows that." I was fascinated with that information. Knowing that he was born on a farm in Jasper County, Illinois, of Scottish parents, I immediately asked, "How was a name from the classics conjured up on a farm in North East Illinois?" "My parents were readers," replied Burl. He told me of learning new songs, and about local culture and heritage in all the different parts of the country. The *Saturday Evening Post* article was titled "America's Troubadour" and, in the 1940's, that really described Burl Ives. I am not a drinker, so I nursed two glasses of wine — a good thing, as it turned out, because we were there the entire afternoon. This was one of the most interesting days of my life.

The *East Of Eden* sound stage shooting period from June through the first ten days of August changed my life around. It was like a train changing tracks. *Eden* officially "wrapped" its shooting on August 9, 1954. Post-production was being finished up, which included Lenny Rosenman's score being put to the film. Jimmy was not involved of course, but it was big for my other close friend, Lenny. The Rosenmans had found a pleasant little house to rent in a very nice section of the San Fernando Valley, close to Warner, called Toluca Lake, which is where Bob Hope had his compound. I would visit Lenny and Adele often and sit at the piano while Lenny composed his *Eden* score, and he would play parts of it for me and ask my opinion for whatever he felt it was worth. I loved it and still believe it was Academy Award worthy.

Lenny kindly invited me to the first recording session where Ray Heindorf and the orchestra were putting his music on film under the "credits." It really was exciting and I could see Lenny was very taken with the moment. I was thrilled for him. We could see the silent film being shown on the screen behind the orchestra, and hear the live music being recorded onto the film. This was a first for me, and a memory that I have always cherished.

Between Lenny and my new friend, however, things were not going swimmingly. I found myself involved in the first of a couple of situations where I noticed a distinct cooling between Jimmy and Lenny.

Photographer Dennis Stock told me the purported reason for the rift. Lenny's version was somewhat different when he mentioned it to me. According to Dennis — and this is one time I am relating a story second-hand — Lenny had bedded Lois Smith while they were neighbors in that apartment building across from the Warner lot. Jimmy had a Victorian moral streak in his make-up. Perhaps it came from his church-going Midwestern upbringing by Ortense and Marcus Winslow.

Adultery, or as Hollywood would term it, "recreational sex," was hardly unknown. But Adele had included Lois in many meals at the family table, and Jimmy's moral sense was deeply offended. So one night Jimmy showed up at the Rosenman apartment — slightly drunk — and berated Lenny in front of Adele and both Dennis and Lois, who were having dinner there. I have to say at this point that I never had a conversation with Jimmy about this, but I did discuss it with another good friend in later years, columnist and author Joe Hyams, and he more or less confirmed the story that Dennis had told me. Lenny mentioned something to me about Jimmy showing up one night, slightly drunk, and that he was "very rude and out of line." Lenny clearly wasn't going to discuss it further, but his friendship with Jimmy was clearly damaged.

In late summer, August of 1954, *East of Eden* was finished. *Rebel Without a Cause* would not begin shooting until March 1955, a period between films of seven months. I was 26 years old. I had a new Buick Century convertible, a really classy car at that time. I was single and lived in a very nice home with a pool overlooking the San Fernando Valley — who could ask for anything more? Additionally, I was a friend of an up-and-coming film actor who was bringing me onto the Warner lot quite often, and I was meeting people I had seen on the screen for years.

The only thing missing was being introduced to, and dating, some of the young lovelies on the Warner lot. I soon learned that Jimmy was not going to aid me in that pursuit at all. Not because of any competitive thing, but rather because Jimmy thought he had to protect me from them. The starlets or actresses in general "weren't my type," and "actresses are unstable," he would advise me. "No, you don't want to get involved with an actress." I wondered what he meant by "unstable," and he said, "You know, they're pursuing their careers, and they are emotional. Regular women are difficult enough. Actresses are more so." But, of course, these rules didn't apply to him because *he* could handle them, and I needed protection. I just laughed this off knowing that if I really wanted to date an actress, I would.

One particular lunch in the Green Room gave me my first clue to Jimmy's attitude towards the subject. He had asked me to come out and have lunch. There was no agenda, just companionship. So I met Jimmy outside the restaurant and we walked in. I glanced around while we were waiting for a table and spied a young actress who had caught my eye in films, and would have liked to date, Karen Sharpe. She was sitting alone and reading, probably a script. When we were seated I mentioned her to Jimmy, "That's Karen Sharpe over there; I like her type." Jimmy didn't even turn to look, he just mumbled, "Yep." So I took it a step further and said, "I wouldn't mind meeting her," and Jimmy said, without even looking up from the menu, "Yep." That was it. Message delivered and understood.

After *Eden* wrapped, Jimmy had time on his hands for the first time since coming back to L.A., so we began to spend more time together at night. Central Hollywood sits between La Brea Avenue on the west and Western Avenue on the east, with two main east-west boulevards running between them: Hollywood Boulevard and Sunset Boulevard. This area contained quite a few live jazz joints — bars with live music. When I say live music, I mean name artists like Nat King Cole and his trio. This was a different part of Hollywood. The Sunset Strip began at Sunset Boulevard and Laurel Canyon as its easternmost border, a corner that housed Schwab's Drug Store and coffee shops like Googies. There was a saying around town in those days that "the working actors went to Schwab's, and the unemployed ones were at Googies."

The old Hollywood establishments had regulars like Lana Turner and Clark Gable and giants like Darryl Zanuck frequenting their own party places, which were mostly all on the Strip: night clubs such as the Mocambo, Trocadero, and Ciro's, or restaurants like The Players, Cock & Bull, Scandia, and The Marquis. Famous exceptions were located in central Hollywood — Musso & Frank, the Brown Derby, Don the Beachcomber, and our regular spot: the Villa Capri.

Chapter Six

A PLACE CALLED THE VILLA CAPRI

After Burl Ives dropped me back at Warners, late in that wonderful afternoon, I stopped by Jimmy's dressing room for a few minutes to finish our visit, and was about to leave when Jimmy asked, "Do you like Italian food?" I immediately thought of spaghetti and meat sauce, which was all I knew about Italian food. "Sure", I answered. Jimmy asked, "Want to meet me at this place in Hollywood where I usually go?" I answered in the affirmative again, and Jimmy told me where it was. I had never gone to an Italian restaurant, per se, even though my folks had taken us to the best eateries in L.A. over the years. Jimmy took me, as we were always to do, through the kitchen from the parking lot, and then into the dining room. We were the only people I know of that Carmine, the chef, allowed to do that. We would joke around with Carmine, a wild Italian, and his crew. We would help ourselves to morsels from the antipasto bins. But this night I was a spectator, and just watched Jimmy interact with the Villa people. We sat down at a waiting booth. The Villa always put a tray of antipasti on every table before even taking the drink order. That was another warm side to the Villa. I looked at the three-tiered serving piece. It contained salami, olives, some kind of fish thing, and calamari. I had never even heard the word "calamari." I looked at the calamari and the calamari looked at me, and we mutually decided to pass. I recognized the salami and the olives and ate them. Jimmy was very relaxed and friendly, greeting almost everyone in the place. We didn't talk much that night, just ate. I was just taking it all in. Oh yes, I ordered pasta with meat balls. I was struck by the fact that the place was pretty full, including the bar, and that almost everyone knew everyone else. Yet the room was warm, homey, and full of celebrities, words that don't go together as a rule. There didn't seem to be an undertone of envy, jealousy or competitiveness like you would find anywhere else Hollywood celebs gathered.

Looking back, it is very difficult to put a reason for the Villa becoming the Villa. Did it just happen; was it because of owner Patsy D'Amore, or was it because Sinatra liked to go there? Or was it the working crew? Probably it was a combination of all of them. In any event, it became very special to the regulars. There was a busboy, Eddie, whose mental capacity was diminished by birth or illness. He bussed the tables, but also greeted everyone at the tables and laughed and spoke loudly. The Villa treated Eddie like a family member, and the regulars all gave him his audience and laughed with him. Jimmy was very fond of Eddie.

The Villa Capri was in Hollywood on McCadden Street, one block east of Highland Avenue and one block North of Hollywood Boulevard. It sat next to another famous and popular eatery, Don the Beachcomber. I was always amused by the fact that the manager of the "Beachcomber" almost always ate dinner at the Villa bar, where Baron, the bartender, held sway.

The Villa was always full of celebs: Patsy D'Amore was a friend of Frank Sinatra, so Sinatra and his pals were in there a lot. But so were many others, like Kim Novak, Vic Damone, and Dean Martin. There were many feature actors, writers, and even well-known songwriters. The Villa also was the spawning ground for soon-to-be famous restaurateurs like Jean Leon of the legendary La Scala in Beverly Hills, Matty Jordan of Matteo's in Westwood, and Dan Tana of Dan Tana's in West Hollywood. All three restaurants were founded by waiters at the Villa Capri, and all three became extremely successful. La Scala was famous on both coasts; President John Kennedy would have

Jimmy & Me

La Scala cater to wherever he was staying when in town. Danny Tana was actually a European soccer player, and an illegal immigrant of 19 years of age who crossed into the U.S. through Canada, and who Patsy more or less adopted, putting him in the small apartment above the Villa Capri. Danny was given whatever job had to be done, what the British call a "dogsbody." Danny, aside from being one of L.A.'s important restaurateurs, became very large in world soccer.

When Jean Leon opened La Scala, he took the chef, Carmine, and the bartender, Baron, with him from the Villa Capri and attracted an upscale Beverly Hills crowd. Matteo's and Dan Tana's attracted a more Damon Runyonesque crowd like jockeys and bookies — people straight out of *Guys & Dolls*. There were nights at La Scala, years after Jimmy's death, when my wife and I sat in the only booth in the main room that wasn't full of celebs. We regularly saw June Allyson and Dick Powell, Milton Berle, Dean Martin and his wife, and George Stevens, the director of *Giant*. La Scala actually was out-Villa-ing the Villa in celebs, but the Villa's great days and the special feeling it gave the regulars would never be matched again.

I cannot mention the Villa Capri without mentioning their maître d' — their official greeter, character of all characters, and Jimmy's future landlord — Nikko Romanos. Nikko was a really funny guy who doubled as an actor in films, and trebled as the duck on Groucho Marx's *You Bet Your Life* television show, one of the most popular on TV. Groucho had a gimmick wherein if the contestant uttered that show's "magic word" for the night, a paper duck would come down from the ceiling with a cash bonus. Sitting beside the duck on a swing would be Nikko, who would then banter with the contestant and Groucho.

I was fortunate to have formed friendships with all of these wonderful guys: Matty, Dan, Jean, and Nikko. And the friendships lived long after Jimmy died. In the '60s, '70s and '80s, I was taking my family and friends to their restaurants, and we were treated like one of their family. My friendship with Jean Leon was closer. Jimmy, Jean, and I had plans for a restaurant, to be run by Jean of course, once Jimmy's new contract was in play. That restaurant would probably have been La Scala. We were still discussing the opening of a restaurant even after Jimmy had died.

I didn't particularly want any part of the restaurant business, but Jimmy absolutely insisted that I had to be a part of any venture of his. I think that's because he knew I would keep everything straight while he, Jimmy, would eat and hang out there, but nothing else. Jimmy did not want to be encumbered with responsibilities and details outside his craft, but he did want to do things and own things.

When I was with Jimmy, we didn't gravitate to the Sunset Strip when we were roaming around at night, aside from The Hamburger Hamlet. La Brea to Western, west to east, is about two miles, that's all. Hollywood Boulevard was a long block above Sunset Boulevard, so from the night spots of the Strip to the jazz joints on Sunset took only a few minutes of driving. (Nobody walks in L.A., not now, not then.) The Hamburger Hamlet, the only one at the time, sat on the eastern end of the Strip just before the Beverly Hills city limits. This was our night time territory, generally speaking. I think I was in Schwab's once with him, and we never went to restaurants other than the Villa. There were no Starbuck's or Peet's in 1954. The Hamlet was intimate while being a really good coffee shop; they had a good menu, and great New York cheesecake. The Hamlet also had a small terrace with a few tables, so you could sit out there and watch the traffic go by on the Strip, or sit in one of the few booths in the booth room. It was a nice cozy actor's environment: decorated in Old English style, with little plaques on the wall, one of which stuck with me because I always seemed to be sitting facing it while Jimmy and Ursula Andress, who Jimmy began dating during the filming of *Giant*, sat under it. I remember it read "Eat the Sides, I Pray You." The Hamlet remained one of my favorite places long after Jimmy's death.

As I've mentioned, Hollywood, in those days, was home to some bars on Sunset Boulevard between Highland and Western Avenue that featured live music. A couple of these places were more like night clubs in that they had name musicians playing there. Even big names. One night, Jimmy and I went to see and hear Nat King Cole. Nat had a big recording hit out called "Too Young," and he had just finished singing another big hit of his, "Nature Boy", when a guy from the crowd yelled out, "Too Young!" And Nat came right back with, "Too loud!" We really got a kick out of this exchange. Another time, Jimmy and I were sitting in a bar on Sunset near Vine listening to some recorded jazz. Jimmy must have known this place because we never went to bars except to hear live music. It also must have been an actors' hangout, as sitting next to me on a stool at the bar, obviously on a date, was the actress Mary Murphy, who had starring roles in major films like *Desperate Hours* with Humphrey Bogart, and *The Wild One* with Marlon Brando. This bar, whose name I can't recall, was mainly a long bar, a rather narrow room with tables along the opposite wall. Soon, a couple of other actors walked in who knew Jimmy. They ordered drinks and we were talking about nothing in particular when one of them mentioned that "Vampira" was having a party. Vampira was the pseudonym for actress Maila Nurmi, a local TV celeb who hosted a regular monster or ghoul movie on Channel 11 every week on TV. One of the guys got the idea of posing as Vice Officers and "raiding" Vampira's party. Jimmy didn't seem very enthusiastic, but he went along with it. As for me, I went reluctantly. I don't like practical jokes; I don't think they are practical, nor are they jokes. I should have had the courage of my convictions, but this was all new to me, and I remember that I wasn't sure what to do. Besides, Jimmy and I were in one car. It wasn't until later when we both had Porsche Speedsters that we went in tandem at night, in our own cars. Vampira knew Jimmy, and they figured she would go along with the gag.

Off we went to Vampira's party, despite my misgivings. As it turned out, I watched rather than actively participated. Maybe I was a little square in Hollywood terms. They stormed through the front door shouting, "Vice! Everybody line up against the wall!" And, strangely enough, everyone did — probably because in those days you automatically respected authority.

Jimmy was not recognizable yet; *Eden* had not been released. The phoney raid included some "pat downs," and I finally told Jimmy we had to call it off when one of our group started to take a female into the bathroom for a more thorough search. Jimmy, I think, was looking for just such an excuse and pulled our "covers." "Okay" Jimmy yelled out, "that's the end of our improv." As the room was filled with actors or acting students, they picked up on Jimmy's message immediately. I clearly remember the thought going through my mind at that instant: "I wish Jimmy had a liability policy." Maila/Vampira thought it was a great joke, or at least played that part. Others laughed more out of relief, I think, than anything else. I don't know about Jimmy, but I never saw Maila again, nor did he ever mention her to me after that night.

It was after this night that I started thinking about the practical things that Jimmy needed in his life. I also felt that our friendship was at a stage where I could suggest moves he needed to make for protection and peace of mind. The first thing I wanted to accomplish was insuring Jimmy against public liability. That would protect him against being sued for purported bodily harm, slipping on his front walk, or other

Jimmy & Me

allegations. I brought it up in 1954, but it wasn't until 1955 that we actually got it done.

Jack Warner was adamant about Jimmy not living on the lot, as no one was allowed to live on the lot. He was driving Jimmy's Hollywood representative Dick Clayton crazy. Jimmy's lead agent was Jane Deacy in New York City, who Jimmy trusted implicitly. But Jane agreed that Jimmy needed an agent on the ground in Hollywood to handle his needs — from setting up dates with starlets to problems with the studio — and she chose former child actor Dick Clayton from the Famous Artists agency. Dick was a very sweet man, and not someone you would think was an agent. We were friends for many years until he passed on.

Dick Clayton happened to have a studio apartment above a garage in the rear of a Hollywood Hills home above Sunset Boulevard, and out of desperation, he turned it over to Jimmy in order to get Jimmy off the Warner lot, and Jack Warner off of his (Dick's) back. Jimmy finally moved off the lot and into the apartment in January 1955.

One early evening that same month, Jimmy came by and said, "Hop in. I want to show you something." So I got into Jimmy's red MG-TD (the car that made a lot of noise but didn't go anywhere), and we drove over Laurel Canyon, down to Sunset, and up to this house above the Strip. Jimmy pulled into the drive and all the way to the rear. We got out of the car and climbed the outside stairs to the apartment. Jimmy said, "This is my new place for a while." I never knew why he brought me there; I think he just wanted me to know where he lived in case I ever wanted to drop by. I recall that the place covered the entire top floor of a two-car garage. It had one very large room that included living space and sleeping space and a bathroom. I don't remember seeing a kitchen, or what passed for a kitchen — but I never ever saw Jimmy even boil water so I really didn't look for one. Now that I think about it, I never saw Jimmy do anything at all in the kitchen he had at Nikko's lodge, either. I remember feeling that Jimmy was definitely not emotionally involved in this place. It looked temporary, felt temporary and Jimmy seemed completely uninvolved. In retrospect, I've come to realize that just about everywhere Jimmy lived once he left the Winslow Farm was temporary.

When we weren't at the Villa Capri, or at The Hamlet, Jimmy and I often went to the movies, especially when he was between films. Not the new releases, but the "Golden Oldies." I have always loved the movies. I can remember the films and, in most cases, the theater I saw them in, and with whom I saw them (if anyone). L.A. in those days was chock full of movie houses: First-run, second-run, even third and fourth-run houses — and older films yet. Jimmy wanted to see films he had an interest in. Not so much for the acting, but for the directing, photography and the cutting. And since these films happened to be among my favorites, we had no trouble agreeing on what to see. This was the time before cable and satellite, so you had to seek out the movie section of the *L.A. Times* to see what was on offer. And let me tell you, there was plenty to choose from. Aside from everything else, we had The Hitching Post on Hollywood Boulevard that showed westerns exclusively, and a movie house on Fairfax Avenue near Beverly Boulevard that showed only silent films. We had everything.

Jimmy and I ferreted out a lot of films during this period: *The Miracle of Morgan's Creek*, *Sullivan's Travels*, *Stagecoach*, *Fort Apache*, *The Palm Beach Story*, *The Man in the White Suit*, *The Lavender Hill Mob*, *Gunga Din*, *The Lost Patrol*, *The Ox-Bow Incident* and *Hail the Conquering Hero*, to name a few. Ironically, we saw a lot of Alec Guinness films, and we were to have an unplanned dinner with Alec Guinness just a couple of days before Jimmy died. I suspect that Jimmy either wanted to or planned to make a comedy and a western in the future.

In the 1950's, the studios were still having world premières of their big pictures as part of their marketing programs, and it was routine for a studio to require young actors and starlets to attend these events for publicity purposes. Jimmy was called upon, sometime between *Eden* and *Rebel*, to attend just such a Hollywood event. Jimmy didn't want to do it, and his body language said as much as soon as he walked up to the interviewer on the red carpet. He was paired, for some studio reason, with a young actress by the name of Terry Moore. Ms. Moore had a few films behind her with second or feature billing, and was the epitome of a young Hollywood player being pushed by a studio, hopefully into stardom.

Ms. Moore did work in a quality film with Frederick March, *Man on A Tightrope*, which centered round a European circus during the Cold War. In the film, Terry Moore was called upon to snap a whip at some lions which, Jimmy told me later, might have stretched her talent. But she did create quite a stir in a press release issued to coincide with the release of the picture. Terry, or her press agent, claimed that "... all that whip snapping during the shooting of the film had added two inches to her noticeable bust," thus setting off a country-wide run on whips.

Be that as it may, I was watching the telecast of the actors on the red carpet, and there is Jimmy, all done up in a tux, and Terry Moore doing her Hollywood première thing in front of the emcee. The interview was short, and Jimmy's première career was over, at least for the time being. Jimmy was intent on sending a message to Warner and their PR department. The emcee turned to Jimmy and asked, "What do you think of Terry Moore?" Jimmy replied, "She keeps a clean dressing room."

Lew Bracker

Pause. Silence. "Ah, thank you very much. Oh, here comes our next interviewee …"

Chapter Seven

WHISPERING IN MY EAR

Jimmy and I became closer as friends after *East of Eden* wrapped, as he had free time for the first time since coming to LA for the film's pre-production. This was a mixed blessing for me, because people began to whisper disparaging comments in my ear about Jimmy. The main source of these whisperings seemed to be people who "knew people" in N.Y., who knew Jimmy earlier in L.A., or when he was broke. These whisperings all indicated a dark and untrustworthy side of Jimmy, and were intended to warn me off. The message was clear: "Get out before he hurts you." The photographer Dennis Stock did a little of this under the guise of a friendly warning following an incident between the two in Palm Springs that I will recount shortly. He wasn't heavy-handed, nor did he press the point, but in little subtle asides, he intimated that I should put the brakes on so I wouldn't get hurt. "Don't get too close" Dennis once said, before he left for France to work on *The Mountain*. "Just play it by ear." The bulk, however, was coming third and fourth-hand. I just stuck to my policy of nodding and not getting into a conversation about my relationship with Jimmy.

I met Dennis Stock through Jimmy. I believe that Dennis had met Jimmy at director Nicholas Ray's bungalow at the Chateau Marmont. Dennis, a highly talented photographer, was in Hollywood on assignment, but after the shoot was over, he decided he wanted to stay on in Hollywood. Dennis told me he wanted to insinuate himself into the movie making business. He was a very well-known photographer and, in fact, shot the most famous of the James Dean lay-outs for *Life Magazine*, but he seemed to be experiencing a young-life crisis. And, brash young man that he was, he actually landed a job at Paramount as "Dialogue Director" on the Spencer Tracy movie *The Mountain* after his initial Hollywood job as script supervisor on *Rebel Without A Cause*, courtesy of Nick Ray. Script supervisor and dialogue director sound great, but the job is simply to follow the script while a scene is being rehearsed or shot, and being ready to feed a line to an actor. Thankfully, considering the wonderful pictures Dennis shot during the rest of his career, he left Hollywood behind. I think it was a combination of the great success of his Dean photos, his lack of real entry into filmmaking, his cooling with Jimmy, and then Jimmy's tragic death that accounted for this.

Dennis and Jimmy went to Fairmount, Indiana (where Jimmy grew up in the Winslow Farm household) for the now famous *Life Magazine* layout in February of 1955. Jimmy asked me if I wanted to go and I said, "No, I would only be in the way," and work was work. Besides, they were going on to New York, where Dennis would continue the shoot and take the Manhattan photos of Jimmy in Times Square. If the trip were to have been just a visit to the farm, I would have gone.

Later, when Dennis was about to go on location for *The Mountain* in the French Alps, he asked if he could leave his Austin-Healey with me so that he wouldn't have to leave it on the street at his apartment. One Saturday morning, I was going to drop by Jimmy's place, and I decided to take Dennis' Healey in order to run the engine a little bit. When I got to Jimmy's, he came out, looked askance at Dennis' car, and said, "I wouldn't use that thing if I were you, because you could have insurance problems if something happened." Now, at times, Jimmy acted like he felt he was my older brother, even though I was a year and a half his senior. Was this an example of Jimmy thinking that he was my mentor or big brother, or was he actually showing some pique or jealousy about my separate friendship with Dennis? By this time, the friendship between Jimmy and Dennis had cooled, and Jimmy was letting me know he didn't trust Dennis anymore.

As I understand it, because this is one of the rare times in this book that I am relying on what I was told (not having actually been there), their rift dates back to the Palm Springs Sports Car Races in March of 1955. Jimmy went down there with Dennis to take some photos and race his Speedster, as he was not yet under studio orders banning his racing.

The trouble appears to have started during that weekend, due to Jimmy seemingly breaching Dennis' code of morality. It centered round an involvement between Jimmy and a young Hollywood aspirant, Lila Kardell, known in Hollywood as Lili. Dennis was shocked and embarrassed and very disapproving, and most likely said as much to Jimmy, who really didn't want to hear it. Something about bending Lila over the sloping hood of Jimmy's new month-old Porsche and going at it in a parking lot, with Dennis as a hapless spectator. Lila Kardell had a reputation around Hollywood, earned or unearned, relating to the casting couch. She was trying to climb the Hollywood ladder any way she could to become a film star. There was definitely nothing serious on Jimmy's side in this relationship, which was short-lived, but Lila may have felt differently. It has occurred to me that maybe Lila was supposed to be with Dennis that weekend. That would certainly have accounted for everything that followed.

Before their own relationship cooled, Lenny never talked to me about Jimmy in a negative way, nor did he ask any questions. He and Adele were well aware of our growing friendship, but never ventured an opinion or a comment. When I was with them, I was with them.

Lew Bracker

As our friendship became closer the vague mutterings and warnings increased in volume. I listened politely and offered no comment. Since Jimmy had done such a thorough job of keeping me away from other people he had known, like Bill Bast and Rogers Brackett, they didn't have my ear, and I didn't read what they wrote after Jimmy's death. I have heard all the stories about Jimmy going both ways sexually. I can only tell you from my experience that Jimmy really liked girls. I also know that Jimmy knew how to survive, and that he had an insatiable curiosity. I can say unequivocally that he never gave me any indication, or reason to think, that he was gay, and we were alone quite a bit at Jimmy's place, our house — and even shared a bedroom once. One of our most recurring conversations was about girls. Someone would have to produce photos, and then prove they weren't doctored to get my attention on this subject.

I wasn't concerned with whatever happened in New York; I wasn't there. Jealousy flourished in Hollywood, and while it appeared to be more pronounced among actors, there was plenty to go around during the studio system era among contract directors and producers. By 1955, I realized that a storm of jealousy surrounded Jimmy in Hollywood, beginning in 1954 after *Eden* wrapped.

Being crowned Jimmy's best friend seemed to have evolved into a Hollywood competition, particularly on *Rebel Without a Cause*, but it paled in comparison to what happened after Jimmy died ... it became a national competition. There were people racing to write books proclaiming themselves to be Jimmy's closest friend and, while they were at it, their publishers pushed them to insert anything racy. Fact or fiction, it didn't matter. For a veritable loner, Jimmy seemed to have an amazing amount of close friends in death.

Jimmy & Me

His relationships with fellow actors rarely developed into friendships. I mentioned earlier that Jimmy didn't get along with his *Eden* co-star Dick Davalos. Similarly, there seemed to be some difficulty between the actor Ben Gazzara and Jimmy. Ben, who I knew personally, was a very gracious guy. He was a good friend of my sister Midge, who was a talented actress studying in New York, and he was very welcoming to me when I visited her in New York in the summer of 1953. It was a Wednesday, and I had gone to see the play *A Hatful Of Rain* starring Ben and Eva Marie Saint. After the show, Ben took me to Sardi's, the famous Broadway restaurant. Another actor in the cast, Henry Silva, joined us, and we spent the entire afternoon there until they had to leave for the evening performance.

By the summer of 1954, Midge had moved back to L.A. She was always worried that Jimmy would drop by the house at the same time that she was there with Ben. When she first brought it up, I asked her about it, but she put me off by saying "Oh, something in New York", and I knew I wasn't going to get any more than that. I figured that Midge now had her own home and family, so the chances of Ben and Jimmy being at the house at the same time were pretty slim. I never did find out what the trouble was between them.

I can only tell you what I know: Jimmy never showed me anything but respect, sincere interest, and absolute equality. In truth, Jimmy sought me out more than the other way around. I never witnessed any of the things whispered to me about Jimmy. Our relationship was very much the same as any other two best friends who like to do a lot of things together, but who also had other interests and pursuits.

I realize now that Jimmy's solitariness sparked the remarks about rudeness and coldness. He was a dedicated member of each cast and crew, but then moved on to the next "family" and film. Jimmy was totally committed to the film he was working on — but then he moved on.

I read in the columns of that period that Jimmy was "rude," "unapproachable," and "monosyllabic." I always wondered, "Who is this stranger I'm reading about?" Jimmy loved to converse, and as I said before, he had an intense curiosity and asked a lot of questions. He laughed a lot if he was comfortable with whomever he was talking to. Sometimes Jimmy would take out his false front-teeth and stick them on the table for shock value. Much of Jimmy was just a young guy, a regular guy, but a guy who was shy at heart, one who had been lonely in some part of his heart since his mother died and was always looking for his own family — a family that no longer existed.

A moment in time that illustrated Jimmy's shyness and the little boy inside happened one day in July of 1955. Jimmy and I were joined in the Green Room at Warner's for lunch by Dick Clayton. During the course of the lunch, Jimmy asked Dick if he could arrange a date with a 20th Century Fox starlet by the name of Virginia Leith. Dick, not understanding the dynamics said, "Sure, I can get her phone number for you. I know she'd love to go out with you." Jimmy said, "No, I mean would you sort of set it up, and then I'll call her." In other words — Jimmy wasn't going to risk rejection.

Dick said he would take care of it, and Jimmy turned to me with an excited smile on his face and said, "Oh boy, Virginia Leith." I remember just looking at him and thinking, "Virginia Leith?" Virginia Leith had appeared in a 20th Century Fox film or two as a featured player, and I had seen her films, but she certainly wasn't my type. I thought Miss Leith would have jumped at the chance of a date with James Dean if Jimmy called out of the blue. And 20th's PR department would have been ecstatic. I was slightly puzzled at Jimmy's excitement because Virginia was not

Jimmy & Me

at all the same type as Ursula Andress, and definitely not like Pier Angeli. I was even more puzzled by Jimmy's reluctance to call her direct. I don't know if he ever took Miss Leith out again, because he never mentioned anything about the date to me, or mentioned Virginia Leith again, but I'll always remember how he was like an excited little boy that day.

As the start of shooting on *Rebel* got closer, Jimmy began to emerge from his shell more and more. He was looking forward to getting back to working on his craft and just being busy. I didn't have to ask him if he wanted to make his own movies; he told me so himself. Jimmy had dreams, but they were not about getting that one great part. He wanted to be so important in Hollywood that he could dictate what movies he was in and/or would make. No one thought that this would come with just two films — not even Jimmy — but I would bet the ranch that Jane Deacy knew as soon as she saw *Eden*.

During *Rebel*, Jimmy began to just drop by at night when they were not shooting, or when shooting ended early. We didn't make dates; we just picked up the phone and asked, "What are you doing?" But Jimmy now just started showing up, mostly after 10:00 p.m.. I wasn't always home, because Jimmy never gave notice, so I was either at a movie or on a date. Jimmy would show up and my mom, hearing the Porsche, would come to the door. Jimmy would shout from the car, "Is Lew home?" When my mom would say "No," Jimmy would just wave and take off. My mom said he always had a girl in the car on these occasions. I would ask what she looked like, and my mom would always tell me, "All I could see was her hair."

The between-films period had come to a close. *Rebel* began shooting at night at an old Hollywood mansion and at the famous Griffith Park Observatory. The *Eden* era had ended for

Lew Bracker

Jimmy and me, and the completely different, darker *Rebel* era was about to begin.

It didn't make an impression on me at the time that Warner was putting Jimmy right into a second film as the star. Jack Warner knew he had a hot property, and he wanted to get another picture out there right away. Jimmy was not getting rich. Warner had a three-picture contract where Jimmy made $6,000 for *Eden* and $9,000 for *Rebel*. He was to earn $21,000 for *Giant*. Of course Jimmy had never seen this much money, and these were 1955 dollars. Still, it was a tremendous bargain for Warner Brothers.

East of Eden opened in L.A in February of 1955 while Jimmy was in New York, so I went down to Hollywood to see the film. My immediate thought as the film ended was, "Jimmy is going to be a big star." I was also thrilled for Lenny because I thought the score was so wonderful. I can tell you that nothing changed for Jimmy and me. Yes, the word was out in town, and probably across the country, that James Dean was the new sensation. But I saw no change in Jimmy, and certainly no change in our relationship. One thing I did notice once or twice when Jimmy and I were driving in his car, was people in other cars pointing at him. So that was a first, but Jimmy seemed not to notice.

Would I have fallen victim to Jimmy's purported dark side over time? I am not clairvoyant, but mark this: sixteen months is a long time in a relationship of any kind to not see most of a person's personality and character traits. I can only tell you that our friendship was closer and stronger than ever on September 30, 1955.

Chapter Eight

THE "DARK" MOVIE

I have always thought of *Rebel Without a Cause* as the "dark" movie. I have my reasons for dubbing *Rebel* with this foreboding sobriquet, some of which occurred after the filming of the movie. Although while it was being shot, I was aware of a distinct atmospheric change whenever Jimmy asked me to visit him and I walked onto the set. The changes were both intangible and physical, but I could certainly feel them. I only visited the set when invited, but that very fact was the core of the problem for one particular young member of the cast, Nick Adams.

Sitting around a movie set is not my favorite thing to do, and since I had never visited the *Eden* set per se, I wasn't even thinking about visiting the *Rebel* set. I certainly wasn't ready for the intrigues and jealousies that came with it. Being on the *Rebel* set at Jimmy's invitation — which, in reality, was really a request — was a unique experience on many levels. Here were the young turks trying to carve out their piece of turf, plus the presence and phenomena of James Dean, the talk of all Hollywood — and I would say their idol as well. Whatever the *Rebel* set was, it was a recipe for deep, if not violent emotions. And I was the target of both jealousy and other irrational and emotional feelings.

There were so many undercurrents and eddies in the waters around the cast: youth, jealousy, awe, antagonism, competition, and talent. You name it — this set had it. Anyone with an ounce of insight would have picked up on these emotions. You could cut the atmosphere with a knife — a dull knife. And I was the innocent cause of a lot of it during and after my first visit on the set.

And let me be clear on this — these are not the only reasons I think of *Rebel* as the dark movie. Jimmy met a violent death at a young age; Natalie met a violent death at a young age, and Sal Mineo was murdered at a young age, while Nick Adams eventually committed suicide — how much darker can it get?

But it wasn't dark at that moment for most of these young actors. In addition to Jimmy, Nick Adams, Sal Mineo, Dennis Hopper, and Natalie Wood went on to success and even stardom. I have no doubt that this was not mere happenstance, and had much to do with talent, but being in James Dean's next film after his sensational introduction in *Eden* was no small matter. Yes, they were talented, but *Rebel*, as history has shown us, was not just another film — it became the battle cry of every teenage generation since its release in 1955.

A young Dennis, a young Sal and even Natalie, a 17-year-old child acting veteran, had to be thrilled to get a credited role in any major feature film, and by the time shooting began and the James Dean buzz was in full voice, these young actors probably couldn't believe their own good fortunes.

I can pinpoint when the *Rebel* story, as it pertains to me, began. It was immediately after the cast and crew returned from location and began shooting on the sound stage. I had never visited the location shooting and so the cast and crew never saw me or heard of me.

Jimmy had called and asked me to keep him company on the set. His way of doing this was to mention, matter-of-factly, "Why don't you drop by tonight?" What he really was telling me was that he would be sitting around a lot because there was

Jimmy & Me

not much he was going to be involved in, and with me there we could talk about girls, cars, the future, and business. I wasn't too thrilled about staying up late, as I still worked for someone else and had to be at the office when it opened in the morning, yet I knew that Jimmy calling me specifically to visit him on the set was not an idle request. And Jimmy had his own reasons, which might have been as simple as companionship.

I arrived on the set that night, my first *Rebel* visit, to find that Jimmy had arranged for two director's chairs to be set off in a corner only a few yards from the set-up, yet away from the cast and crew. I realized early on that this was a clear message to all others that we were not to be disturbed. That the space between us and the set was no man's land and was not to be invaded. No one came near us that evening, not even director Nick Ray. Ray would call Jimmy over if he needed him.

I say no one came near us, but one person did, an old family friend and top photographer, Gene Kornman, who was hired by Warner Brothers to do all of the still work for the publicity department on *Rebel*. Gene Kornman was a personal friend of my dad, and a really nice person. He was also one of Hollywood's top photographers, having taken the photos of Hollywood legends for a couple of decades. Gene used to come up to our ranch every summer, park his trailer on the beach, and enjoy life. He would also go around the ranch taking great pictures and giving them to my dad.

In fact, when I came home from the Army in August of 1953, Gene invited me to lunch at 20th Century Fox where he was working on a Marilyn Monroe/Robert Mitchum movie, *The River of No Return*. We had lunch and then got into Gene's car and drove out to the back-lot, which is now Century City, to watch the shoot. As it turned out, neither star was there because they were shooting some stunt man stuff of a gun fight. We watched for about 45 minutes, and then made the return trip to the studio and my car. On the narrow road back, another car was coming our way. Gene recognized the ordinary Chevy coupe and pulled over. The car came abreast and stopped, and Marilyn Monroe said "Hi Gene". Gene introduced me as having just come home from the Army in the Far East, and as the son of a friend. Marilyn gave me a big smile and said, "Welcome home." I thanked her, and then she asked Gene about some picture she wanted, and said, "I have to get back to the set." She looked at me and said "I'm glad you're home Lew, safe and sound." I replied, "You sound like my mother," and Marilyn Monroe laughed and pulled away.

So of course Gene came over and gave me a big hello when he spotted me. He made no notice of the fact that I was sitting with James Dean. By that I mean it came as no surprise to him. That was Gene Kornman. Jimmy seemed quite surprised that Gene and I knew each other, though.

Gene polite as ever, asked me if he could take a picture of Jimmy and me. I didn't know what to say, so I looked at Jimmy, and Jimmy said "Sure." Those Kornman pictures are two of my most prized possessions (See back cover of this book.).

On my subsequent visits to the *Rebel* set those two chairs were always in the same spot and the off-limits designation was in full force.

By isolating us from the cast and crew, Jimmy stoked the fires of jealousy and disappointment in others who I didn't even know, and had never met. At that point, I was completely unaware of any hostility or animosity towards me. To my knowledge, Dennis Hopper, Sal Mineo and Natalie Wood harbored no ill will towards me, but were very curious as to who I was and where I fit in Jimmy's life. Especially after they all witnessed

Jimmy & Me

Gene Kornman invading our territory, and even taking some pictures with Jimmy's obvious willingness.

That left Nick Adams.

As I mentioned earlier, I was well aware that while working on a film, Jimmy was very much a part of the film family, but once the film was finished he was gone; he had moved on to his new film family. As you can imagine, as fragile as an actor's psyche is, this caused hurt and disappointment in some cases. Those people had misread Jimmy — they didn't understand that his professional life and his personal life were two very distinct spheres. They took Jimmy's friendliness on the set for real friendship, and had no understanding of Jimmy's defense mechanism. In Jimmy's short career, the only real friendship with a star he seemed to be willing to allow was with Liz Taylor.

The cast of *Rebel* was a young and talented class: Jimmy was 24; Natalie was only 17, but having grown up in the movie business, she was going-on-30. Corey Allen was 21, Dennis Hopper was 19, Sal Mineo was 16, and Nick Adams was 24. Aside from the anxieties of being young actors with all the insecurities that come with it, the recipe on *Rebel* included the unspoken competition to be Jimmy's best friend. Nick Adams was a talented young actor. He was also quite a disturbed person, an opinion confirmed by his future actions. Nick harbored real dislike and jealousy towards me because of Jimmy — or, more to the point, because of my relationship to Jimmy — and our obvious closeness.

I soon learned that Nick thought that he was the anointed one who was going to be Jimmy's best friend, and therefore #1 in the youth gang that was the cast of *Rebel*. Nick did not handle rejection – or even disappointment – well. At the age of 36, he overdosed on prescription drugs at a time when his career was doing well, he had a wife and daughter, and he starred in a TV Western series, ironically titled *The Rebel*.

I was on the lot for another lunch with Jimmy. After lunch, we were standing around outside the Green Room when Nick Adams showed up. Jimmy still did not introduce us, but it didn't matter because Nick, completely ignoring me, started talking to Jimmy a little too loudly and laughing in a forced manner. Jimmy was not rude. He muttered a few things acknowledging the conversation, but was plainly putting up with Nick and not wanting him there. With a nod to Nick from Jimmy, we started back towards the sound stage. Nick walked along keeping up his effort, but eventually fell silent. In truth, it was sad. Nick needed acceptance even more than most actors.

The first time I was on the set, Jimmy didn't work because they were filming the back shoot of the scene where Corey Allen goes over the cliff in the game of "chicken." Specifically, they were shooting Natalie at the edge of the cliff looking over in horror. We were watching, but there wasn't much to watch. Natalie's stand-in, Faye Nuell, stood at the end of what looked like the precipice that Corey Allen drove over when his jacket got caught on the door handle. They checked the lighting and the camera marks, and then Natalie stepped in so that the cameras could shoot her looking over the edge in horror. Since we couldn't talk during shooting, we just watched.

The second night's visit provided the memorable experience of seeing Jimmy really prepare and work out a tough scene. This was the scene at the latter part of the movie where Sal Mineo is killed by the police, and Jimmy cries out in anguish, "I've got the bullets!" indicating that Sal's gun was not loaded. This visit was the opposite of my first visit, in that Jimmy was working and it was a difficult scene to get right. I didn't count the takes, but it must have been over a half dozen on the one line "I've

Jimmy & Me

got the bullets." Jimmy tried it various ways, but wasn't satisfied. In between takes, he and director Nick Ray would discuss the scene. Even the crew got into the act, offering their own opinions. Finally, Jimmy did another take, after perhaps three hours of trying, and he and everybody liked it. Nick called "print."

I have heard and seen it written that Jimmy was the real director of *Rebel*. Not true. I witnessed Nick Ray and Jimmy conferring on individual scenes before shooting. It looked to me like it was collaboration insofar as Jimmy's part was concerned. I did not witness any fireworks between Nick and Jimmy. They were pretty much on the same page; Nick directed the movie, and worked with Jimmy on his scenes.

Jimmy worked long and hard that night on the "bullets" scene, trying it with different inflections until he got what he wanted. Nick, for his part, was very patient and cooperative and in the end, rode with Jimmy until Jimmy was satisfied.

The opening scene of *Rebel*, with Jimmy in the gutter playing with a toy mechanical monkey, was all Jimmy. It was his idea and his direction. By that I mean that Jimmy read the script and already knew he was going to get down in the gutter. Playing with the toy monkey was a great idea, and few actors, if any, would risk a toy stealing the attention of the audience. But to Jimmy, the character and the initial setting of the story was more important.

During the filming of *Rebel*, Nick Ray lived in a bungalow at the famous Chateau Marmont on the Sunset Strip. Ray would hold Sunday afternoon soirées inviting his friends and co-workers. I was never there, because Jimmy went to a couple, and then quit going (most likely because it either bored him and/or his moral streak was at work). Both Jimmy and Lenny told me that Natalie was in attendance all the time because she was practically living with Nick Ray. Actually, Lenny told me Natalie was Nick Ray's mistress. This open secret caused a lot of consternation even in Hollywood. I guess that is why some early regulars of the Nick Ray Sunday afternoon soirées dropped out, and the event eventually faded out.

It wasn't always dark on the set of *Rebel*. I wasn't there that night, but both Jimmy and Dennis Stock told me this story: On a night of sound stage shooting, the make-up and wardrobe people conspired to run a practical joke on Nick Ray. It centered on Natalie Wood who was, let us say, a little light in the bust department. Natalie was attired in a sweater and skirt for her role, so the set up was perfect. In make-up, before she was due on the set, they stuffed a 36-C bra and put it on Natalie. When she came on the set her bust preceded her by six inches. Nick Ray had a fit, but the cast and crew had a big laugh.

Rebel began shooting on March 30, 1955, and finished on May 25, 1955. Out of the young cast, Jimmy — of course — was a star. But Natalie rose to stardom, as did Dennis Hopper. And Sal Mineo starred in a couple of films. Nick Adams certainly attained a good measure of success.

The ending of *Rebel* brought with it a large dose of personal disappointment for Nick Adams. Nick could not let go of Jimmy, and sent him post cards from wherever he was to Jimmy, who was filming *Giant* in Marfa. I know because I found a couple of them on Jimmy's desk after his death.

Chapter Nine

A "GIANT" HEADACHE

It was a day in early March of 1955. *Rebel* had not yet finished shooting, and as far as the studio was concerned, George Steven's *Giant* was going to be Jimmy's next film. Actually, the studio had confirmed Jimmy for the film on March 17. There was one small problem: Jimmy hadn't fully signed on yet in his own mind.

I know it has been written that Jimmy lobbied for this role, but quite a bit of nonsense has been written about Jimmy. He did tell me he was going to do *Giant* next, but Jimmy was well aware of George Steven's autocratic ways on the set, and so he was playing a little game with George Stevens and Jack Warner in order to signal that he wasn't a pawn. On the other hand, Jimmy respected Stevens' ability as a great filmmaker. Jimmy chose to place me square in the middle of this little tug o' war.

That morning in March 1955, I got a call from Jimmy: "Can you come out for lunch today? It's important." With no more information than that, no indication as to why we were meeting, I tended to think that it had something to do with business and organizational plans. I could not have been more incorrect.

I arrived at the Green Room at the appointed time, and Jimmy was sitting alone in a booth. I do believe it was the same booth in which we first met. Jimmy asked me to sit beside him because we were being joined by two other gentlemen. This alone was really a first. Now I was seriously curious. Jimmy didn't offer any more information than that, so I knew something was in the air. I thought that he was surprising me with something he was going to do or to buy, and we were meeting with the principals involved. I figured that maybe he was going to buy a Ferrari, or that he wanted me to listen to some business proposition and give him my advice. I was not prepared for who the gentlemen turned out to be, and why they were there. And definitely not why I was there.

It was only about five minutes before the two men – producer Henry Ginsberg and iconic director George Stevens — arrived. Jimmy introduced me by name, but never told them who I was or what I was doing there. And since I had come from the office, I was wearing a suit and tie and looked like a young executive. We shook hands all around, but Stevens and Ginsberg looked right at me, expecting to get some explanation or reason for my presence. They didn't get either, so they fully accepted my presence, probably in the belief that I was one of Jimmy's agents or his manager. I had the distinct feeling that my name went right by them on the introduction, and they both were trying to remember it. For someone who was not even a film "extra," and never thought I would be having lunch with one of Hollywood's most famous filmmakers and one of Warner's biggest producers, I was feeling pretty damned important. It was funny actually, because these two powerful film moguls were thrown completely off their game right at the start — Jimmy's strategy all along.

As the conversation got around to *Giant*, which it did almost immediately, regarding Jimmy's major role opposite Liz Taylor and Rock Hudson, the reason for the meeting became clear to me. They were selling Jimmy on the film, but wanted to establish who would be in charge — something Jimmy figured out in advance.

Jimmy & Me

They both went on about how it would stretch Jimmy because his character ages in the movie, and this was his first opportunity to portray a Western-type character.

I caught on quickly that they were selling the role and that Jimmy had been showing some reluctance to making the film. My natural instincts told me that my role was to follow Jimmy's lead from the introduction, or lack of it. I was there just to be there, with a serious straight face, looking intense, and looking right at them. And that is what I did all through the lunch meeting.

They wanted Jimmy to know who was going to be boss. Jimmy wanted to even the odds and basically throw them off balance. And it worked. Stevens or Ginsberg would say something about the film and/or the role of Jett, and Jimmy would glance at me! As if I were his guru. Before long, both Stevens and Ginsberg began looking at Jimmy and then at me when they were talking. I really bothered them because I represented the biggest fear in Hollywood — they didn't know who I was, or how much power I had, so I had to be reckoned with, and they had to divide their attention. They weren't taking any chances. Jimmy loved it. He wasn't going to let Hollywood bigwigs, especially George Stevens, gang up on him, and this was Jimmy's way of screwing up their plan. Jimmy looked like the proverbial cat that had swallowed the canary as we left the cafe, with that little half-smile/smirk on his face. Jimmy knew all along he was going to do *Giant*, but he wanted to send his own message.

Jimmy was to use this maneuver later in our relationship, but not on such an important occasion. One night Lenny, Adele, Lois Smith, and Jimmy dropped by the house for coffee and my mother's wonderful baking. I hadn't talked to Jimmy that day and we had no plans. I was really thinking of going to a movie that had just opened. Evidently, Adele had talked to my mom earlier in the day and was invited for coffee after dinner. They were on their way to audit an acting class in Hollywood taught by a very good character actor, Jeff Corey. During the coffee and cake session, Lenny said, "Come with us to the class." "Are you kidding?" I asked, "I'm no actor. I'll probably take in a flick." But then even Lois Smith urged me with, "Come with us. You don't have to do anything but watch. That's what I am going to do." And then Jimmy added, "Yeah, come on, and we'll do something after." So I relented.

In those days I almost always wore a well-worn dark brown leather jacket and jeans or slacks when not working. Jimmy, prior to *Rebel*, wore a black leather jacket and jeans or ducks, or a windbreaker; he was really into T-shirts, so we both looked like "actors." We created quite a stir when we walked into the class. *Eden* hadn't been released yet, but word on Jimmy certainly had been, and Lois was known as a talented young Broadway actress who had a featured role in *Eden* and was already scheduled to make another picture, this time with Greer Garson. So it was like we were visiting royalty to a class of aspiring actors.

Again, Jimmy never introduced me, and the fact that I just sat and watched, saying nothing to anyone through the entire class, only assured them that I was a new somebody. Jimmy did take part in an "improvisation" when asked by Jeff Corey. Corey was obviously pleased and flattered that Jimmy and Lois had chosen to visit his class, and he kept looking at me assuming that I must also be a top New York talent come to Warner Brothers. After all, I was with James Dean and Lois Smith.

The improv consisted of just Jimmy and another male actor. Jimmy started it out and you could see that his fellow participant was startled if not floored by Jimmy's choice. By definition, an improvisation has no script for the actors to rely on. They just

Jimmy & Me

take off and wing it. In this improv, it was just Jimmy and another actor. I don't remember much about it except that Jimmy bolted from the starting gate with conflict. He completely overwhelmed the poor guy trying to play opposite him. He wowed everyone with his improv, but was even more impressive later when Jeff Corey held a post-mortem on the improv and asked the class to quiz the actors who had taken part in it. But Jimmy turned the tables on them when they performed, as he asked questions about their thought processes, their characters, and many other "acting" questions-cum-criticisms. At one point, Jeff Corey was so amazed at the depth of Jimmy's questions that he asked, "Who are you, the D.A.?"

After the class, everyone was wending their way towards their cars, but Jimmy hung back to thank Jeff for the class. Jeff, of course, would have loved to have Jimmy join, but Jimmy wasn't interested at that particular time. Jeff then turned to me and asked, "How about you?" All I said was, "No, thank you."

The George Stevens lunch was my introduction to the *Giant* era, and it was to go downhill from there. *Giant* was a constant battle between Stevens and Jimmy. Jimmy was not the cause of the movie going more than 100 days over schedule, but his battles with Stevens did contribute to the problem. I am sure that Steven's penchant for a lot of retakes didn't sit well with Jimmy.

Once Jimmy was committed to *Giant*, his natural work ethic took over. He wanted to learn as much as he could about anything that would help him understand the people in the story and the person directing the film. He called me one evening and said, "We have to go see a movie. I found an old Stevens film at an oldie theater on Vermont." Off we went to see *Gunga Din*, which is still a favorite of mine. As usual, Jimmy didn't talk shop with me. We went to the Villa Capri and talked about other things. I went to see *Gunga Din* because I loved the film as a movie goer. Jimmy went to dissect each shot, everything the director had done, and why.

The cast and crew of *Giant* left for Marfa, Texas, once Jimmy was free of *Rebel*. The Texas location shooting took about thirty days, with everybody returning to the Warner lot by the end of June. I had no communication with Jimmy during that time, which was not unusual. Because of his busy movie schedule in the short time I knew him, it was not uncommon for Jimmy and me to go a few weeks without speaking to each other. I didn't expect to hear from him, so I wasn't privy to whatever went on in Texas. I did hear from Jimmy about how, in his usual fashion, he talked to old-timers in the area about land, farming, ranching, and everything else he could pick from their brains. It seems that one old rancher told Jimmy, showed him really, how they used to pace off land in order to determine the size in question.

George Stevens didn't take directing suggestions from actors, so his reaction was quite different. When Jimmy improvised with what he had recently learned from the Marfa, Texas ranchers — how they used to measure off their properties — Stevens wasn't happy. In *Giant*, when Mercedes McCambridge's character "Luz" dies and leaves a parcel of land to Jimmy's "Jett," the next scene shows Jimmy "pacing off the land" just like the rancher showed him. According to Jimmy, Stevens had other ideas, leading to one of their constant arguments over how a scene should be played. Obviously, Jimmy won, and it is one of the highlights of the film.

While editing this book, and in my present mode of re-examining everything in my James Dean experience, I opened a briefcase that I hadn't opened in at least 40 years. I knew, more or less, what was in there: the newspapers from Fairmount on the day Jimmy died, and on the day he was buried, but I didn't recall anything else. It was time to look. And I found an

Jimmy & Me

interview with James Dean conducted by Phillip K. Schauer, Entertainment Editor of the *Los Angeles Times*, dated November 7, 1954. I remembered this as one of the items I had taken off of Jimmy's desk when I went to clear out his apartment a few days after the accident, but I never read it. It contains a quote from Jimmy that explains quite a bit about his approach to his craft, and his problems with George Stevens on *Giant*:

"I hate anything that limits progress or growth. I hate institutions that do this, a way of acting that limits a way of thinking."

While the cast and crew were in Texas, I was going through a process that was to change my life considerably. I would drive around L.A. in my Buick convertible, and keep thinking about racing through the canyons of the Hollywood Hills — Laurel, Coldwater, Benedict, and all the rest — in a Porsche. The more I thought of it, the more the idea spread in my mind, until I ended up selling the Buick and buying a pretty red Porsche Speedster with a cane interior in June of '55, just eight months after I bought the Buick. I simply went down to Europa Motors in Studio City and bought the only one they had.

The *Giant* crew came back from Texas for interior shooting for July — and what a July it was going to be. And not just regarding *Giant*, but also for Jimmy and me. So much would go on, and so many conversations about the future would take place. We saw each other often. Jimmy would invite me to visit the set and/or to have lunch, and he began coming up to our house regularly. In retrospect, I think the most important single happening was Jimmy becoming a part of my family. It was the most important shift in our entire relationship.

Thus began the summer of '55.

Chapter Ten

"CISCO"

Do you believe in a "sixth sense" or premonitions? I do because, as my daughters would tell you, I have had accurate premonitions all my life. And what I am about to tell you is absolutely true.

One night I was at home at around eight o'clock with nothing planned, and I suddenly had this feeling that the crew of *Giant* had returned from Texas. Nobody told me, I just felt it. I now was the proud owner of a Porsche — looking for any excuse to go across Mulholland and then down one of the canyons, or just down Laurel Canyon. For those not familiar with Los Angeles, the entire West side is divided by a mountain range, from Hollywood to the beach. Mulholland Drive runs across the top of the range and is intersected by canyons with expensive homes. Our house sat between Coldwater Canyon on the west and Laurel Canyon on the east. If I wanted to go to the Strip, I took Laurel Canyon. If my destination was Beverly Hills, I took Coldwater. If I was headed further west, I took Sepulveda or Beverly Glen. It was all very convenient. But that was not what this was about. I remember the feeling like it was last night.

I had only one thing on my mind, and that one thing was to drive over Laurel Canyon to the Sunset Strip, and down the Strip towards Beverly Hills, where I was certain I would meet up with Jimmy. So I took off over Laurel for West Hollywood knowing we would meet up. I turned west towards Beverly Hills on Sunset to go by Ernie McAfee's Ferrari place (backed by William Holden) and then cruise past the Hamlet.

Jimmy & Me

I didn't have to drive any farther than McAfee's, which was only about 1/2 mile down Sunset. And there was Jimmy and a girl holding hands and looking at the Ferrari in the window. Jimmy's Speedster was parked in front. I spotted the Porsche first, and then the couple window shopping. The Porsche motor has a distinctive sound and there weren't many of them around in '55, so Jimmy heard my Porsche right away and turned to look. I pulled up in front of the showroom and Jimmy was peering, but couldn't tell who was driving. When I climbed out — and you *did* climb in and out of a Porsche — Jimmy was astonished. He didn't know what to say. He blurted out, "What did you do?" Followed by, "I just got back and was going to call you tonight."

Jimmy was very happy to see me, even excited. "We just got back from Texas," he told me. "Actually, day before yesterday, and I slept most of that day." He couldn't get over my selling my big convertible and getting into a Porsche. He was really quite animated, and I now realize he was also really pleased about the step I had taken. I don't know to this day if Jimmy ever thought about his influence, or at least his introducing me to the world of Porsche, as he never talked about it. But I know one thing — Jimmy knew he planted the seed.

After his initial shock over my shedding my Detroit Iron skin and now living in a Porsche skin, Jimmy introduced me to the girl he was with as Ursula Andress, and said that she was under contract to Paramount. Actually, Jimmy had just met her upon his return from Texas, so this might have been their first date! Later, after Jimmy's death, Paramount dropped her contract at option time. I always wondered whatever became of her (said with sarcasm). Ursula, for her part, had been smiling and looking at me all this time, and I believe she was pleased and somewhat surprised by Jimmy's reaction to seeing a friend. I thought at the time that this was apparently a new experience for her to see Jimmy react in this way. But now I know that she was just learning who Jimmy was. "Let's go up to the Hamlet so we can talk," Jimmy said, and so we did. Ursula was quiet, very pleasant, and an interested spectator.

Jimmy was intrigued by the fact that I knew I would run into him that evening after I told him the story. As with everything, Jimmy was curious about my premonitions. Actually, it went beyond curiosity. "What do you feel when you get one of these premonitions? Do you see a picture or hear anything? Are you ever asleep and it wakes you up?" The questions came fast and furiously. I said, "I just get these strong feelings about something, almost out of nowhere. I'm always awake, and sometimes visualize someone calling me and telling me some important news and I even know the words they will say." Jimmy had a strong interest in mediums, the occult, and séances. All I could tell him is that I sometimes get these strong visions or premonitions, if you will, and then what I have "seen" seems to happen. I still go through this today, but it is usually about me or one of my daughters.

I found that I liked Ursula, that she was a very nice quiet girl, unassuming and warm towards me — and inclusive. Yet underneath all of that, I felt that she was strong and strong-willed in so far as getting where she wanted to go. Ursula certainly knew where she wanted to go, and what she was going to do when she got there. Jimmy alluded to this in a later conversation. He told me, "Ursula can take care of herself. After all, she grew up during the war in Europe."

Jimmy and I talked Porsches of course, a subject Ursula had no interest in, but she was studying the interaction between us with interest. She later told me she had never seen Jimmy even come close to being that open and warm with anyone else. I was destined to spend time with Ursula over the next three months.

Jimmy & Me

The next day Jimmy called me to come over to Warner and have lunch, that he had something to show me. So once again I journeyed out to the studio. We had lunch, but Jimmy wouldn't tell me what it was he had to show me. I assumed that after lunch we would be going back to Jimmy's dressing room, or he was going to show me another car he bought. Instead he surprised me by taking me to his Speedster. "Get in," he said. "Where are we going?" I asked, but Jimmy just put that smirk on his face — played mysterious — and didn't answer.

We got into Jimmy's Porsche and drove further down the street towards Glendale, Griffith Park, and the Pickwick Stables, where people rented horses to ride the bridle paths of Griffith Park. I laughingly asked Jimmy, "Are we going riding? I'm not dressed for it!" Jimmy just gave me that half-smile and parked the car. He got out and motioned for me to get out of the car. "Follow me." I did.

We came up to the horse stalls and the exercise track and Jimmy said, "Wait here." Now I was really curious, as Jimmy went to one of the stalls and came out leading a big buckskin horse. He said proudly, "This is Cisco." I said, "Nice." And Cisco was nice, with a black mane and tail, but I was still mystified as to why Jimmy was showing me this horse. And then Jimmy said, "He belonged to a Western stunt man. He can do tricks, and I bought him!" I was more than a little nonplussed. "What do you mean you bought him?" I couldn't get my head around what Jimmy was telling me — I mean, Jimmy lived above a garage! But Jimmy was really enthusiastic about all this and insisted on showing off as he made Cisco bow for me. I remember thinking, "What the hell!"

I love horses. I grew up with horses in Arizona, and rode since I was a kid, but owning a horse in the middle of L.A. is like having an elephant in a Manhattan apartment. And it is just about as expensive. I told Jimmy that boarding and feeding Cisco at a stable would more than equal the rent on his place above the garage, and that was only if you don't have any vet bills, an unlikely scenario. "And when are you going to be able to come by and exercise the animal? Horses need exercise and can't stand in a stall all day." All these practical questions just came tumbling out. I didn't mean to throw cold water on Jimmy's enthusiasm. I didn't mention the fact that Jimmy was not the ideal candidate to have taken on this responsibility, although I certainly thought it.

As we talked it became clear that Jimmy was already feeling the burden of responsibility, not to mention buyer's remorse, and that he felt guilty that Cisco was cooped up in a stall and wasn't getting exercise, among other things. He began fretting about what to do.

Jimmy didn't know about the Ranch we owned, the El Capitan, 17 miles north of Santa Barbara on the coast with 2 1/2 miles of beachfront. The subject had never come up. I said, "We have a ranch north of Santa Barbara. We have some horses, a big corral and barn, and some ranch hands to look after them. I go up there when I can and ride. We can put Cisco up there. He will get exercise and be well taken care of." I told Jimmy I just wanted to clear it with the ranch foreman to make sure there was room for Cisco, but I was certain there was.

Jimmy couldn't believe it. "You've got a ranch?" Now it was Jimmy's turn to be nonplussed. First of all, he was blindsided by the revelation that I knew horses, rode them, could handle them, and that I was "a man of the soil" so to speak — like him. And Jimmy realized that this was an answer to a prayer. He could put Cisco up on a real ranch and never have to worry about him again.

Jimmy & Me

He asked, "You would do that?" I said. "Sure I would, no problem at all. The ranch could probably use another horse anyway, and I'll ride him myself." It was as if I had lifted a blacksmith's anvil off of Jimmy's shoulders. I told my dad that night about Jimmy's problem, and he said he'd arrange it. My dad called the ranch foreman who said "no problem," and in fact they could use another riding horse, and a free one is even better.

When I told Jimmy it was a go, he asked, "How soon can we do this?" "As soon as your schedule permits, just let me know and we're off." The very next weekend saw us taking my fancy Buick convertible, putting a trailer hitch and a horse trailer that Jimmy rented from Pickwick onto the back, loading Cisco and heading for the ranch.

With the trailer it was about a three-hour trip, so we got there in the late afternoon. The foreman and a couple of hands were waiting for us. Jimmy and I had quite a revealing conversation on the way up — at least as far as Jimmy learning more about me was concerned. I told him that from time to time I have gone up to the ranch just to ride the hills. Jimmy asked, "Did you phone ahead so they would have a horse ready for you?" and I said, "No, I would just go up to the corral, get a rope, rope one of the horses (usually Skunk), bridle and saddle him, and take off."

Jimmy had just spent a month in Texas learning rope work, riding and being a cowboy, so he was flabbergasted. He thought I was just a city boy. I explained to Jimmy that I was riding in Arizona when I was eight and that I had been around horses all of my life. I think Jimmy looked at me somewhat differently after that trip.

Lew Bracker

The foreman had been alerted, so he and two hands were waiting for Cisco. They unloaded him and turned him loose in the corral. To me, Cisco seemed happy to be out of the stall and with his kind. He definitely was happy to be out of the trailer. Jimmy was positively ecstatic.

On the way back to L.A., Jimmy was animated and very talkative. He asked questions, most all of them about my family. He wanted to know all about my mom and dad and my aunts and uncles. He was very interested in how close our extended family was, and in my dad's very interesting career, which included working on the Panama Canal and selling WWI surplus equipment to the Juarez followers during the Mexican Revolution. Later that summer Jimmy would talk to my dad and ask him directly about his adventures.

When we finally got back to L.A., we got rid of the hitch and trailer and went straight to the Villa Capri to have dinner, with Jimmy still talking about how great it was that Cisco was on the ranch. I know Cisco was an impulsive purchase for Jimmy. He was excited by the idea of buying the horse, but as usual failed to consider all of the after-purchase ramifications and responsibilities. That night Jimmy was enjoying the best of both worlds. He technically owned Cisco; he knew Cisco was in his element, and that he would be well-cared-for. And Jimmy didn't have to do anything about it.

Jimmy never saw Cisco again, but after all, he lived only a few months after that trip to the ranch. No one can say that he wouldn't have had he lived longer. But the fact remains — Jimmy never went back to the ranch — even though we were only ten miles away when we were in Goleta for my first race weekend.

Jimmy & Me

Cisco lived a good horse's life on the ranch. I would go up there on occasion and ride him even into the mid-sixties. I would ride him in the hills and on the beach. I used to take my daughter Alison on Cisco when she was only a year old. That is how gentle Cisco was, and I used to tell Alison it was "her horsey." I also took my daughter Lesley for rides on Cisco in 1964 when she was less than a year old. These rides were always on the beach in front of the beach cabin. I came to believe that Cisco didn't want to be a performer, and that he wanted to be just a family horse. He seemed to know that he was carrying a very young child. He was so careful and gentle when I had one of the girls with me.

From what people have told me, there have been many rumors as well as totally misinformed stories about Cisco in the Dean books — but this is the true story. Cisco was buckskin, not a palomino, and Jimmy never sold him to anyone. For all intents and purposes, Cisco was mine from 1955 on, and was stabled at the El Capitan Ranch. I rode him many times over a ten year period and he was well-cared-for. And — I suppose from a horse's standpoint — led a fine life once we got him out of that stall in Burbank.

I never rode Cisco without thinking of that day when Jimmy unveiled his new purchase to me at Pickwick Stable. How excited and proud he was that day, and how he wanted me to see Cisco and show off his tricks to me. On that day, Jimmy was a kid with his first pony. Some pony! On that day that I first saw Cisco, I saw a big horse. And showing it to me was a little boy – Jimmy.

Chapter Eleven

TWO GUYS AND TWO PORSCHES

Jimmy never forgot my opinion of the MG. He concluded a deal with Competition Motors in November of 1954 to trade his MG-TD on a deal for a Porsche Super 1500, but he had to wait for delivery until February of 1955.

I believe it was the next weekend, after the Stevens lunch, that Jimmy came up to the house at around two in the afternoon in what looked to me like an inverted bathtub on wheels. I asked, "What is that?" and Jimmy told me it was a Porsche Speedster Super 1500, and that he had just bought it. "Hop in." I did, and he took off out of the driveway, over to Laurel Canyon and then south over Laurel to Sunset Boulevard. Laurel Canyon was a great road for Porsches or any sports car. It is winding and you are going up and up or down and down. I remember continuing to look over my shoulder because the engine was in the rear, a new experience for me, and I thought a police motorcycle was behind us. I kept staring at the Spartan interior: there was no radio, no windows, only plastic side curtains, and a knob on the floor to turn on the "heater" (which was really just hot air off the exhaust). The thing didn't even have a gas gauge or a clock.

We ended up going all the way out to Trancas Beach, almost half-way to Ventura, stopping for lunch at the old Malibu Cafe before heading back. All the way, Jimmy talked about the Porsche and its cutting-edge design by Dr. Ferdinand Porsche, whose grandson I was to meet 56 years later in Monterey, California. Jimmy was hugely enthusiastic about the car, its aerodynamic design, air-cooled, non-radiator engine, and its reverse-camber rear wheels. I just kept looking at the bare bucket seats, ragtop that you could put up or down with one hand. And no radio.

Jimmy's Porsche had so little effect on me that I sold my Olds convertible and bought a new Buick Century convertible with all the interior delights of the day. That's where I was at in my car thinking at the time. Owning one of these strange things didn't even enter my mind. I was conscious, though, of how the little car cornered, and how much faster and maneuverable it was than what sports car enthusiasts called "Detroit Iron" at the time.

On the way back, Jimmy kept on and on, telling me about all the Porsche's virtues, and how he was going to get into sports car racing. I knew nothing about sports car racing or any of the organizations concerned with racing. I simply didn't have any interest, although I evidently did in my subconscious. I must have been very much aware of how this little bug was eating up the Laurel Canyon curves and how Jimmy was able to put his big toe in the water, so to speak, by putting the Porsche into a four-wheel drift on a curve. I was fascinated by the fact that you drove the Porsche by the tachometer (I had never even seen a tach in a car) instead of the speedometer. So, unrecognized by me at the time, Jimmy had opened a new door in my life and led me through it. He had planted a seed that was to bear fruit within a couple of months.

I had such a lack of interest on a conscious level in sports cars and racing that I didn't go to any of Jimmy's three races. That was just something he did while I did something else. Of course Jimmy told me all about his first-ever race at Palm Springs. "Man, they dropped the flag, and I just put the pedal to the floor." Palm Springs was a course with a long back straight and a fairly long front straight with only two sets of "esses," one off the front straight and one off the back straight, so it was a fairly simple course where the faster cars had a big advantage. "I got through the turns, but I was all over the place" Jimmy added. "I just wanted to get to the flag as fast as I could." In his short career, that seemed to be Jimmy's objective. Of course Jimmy would have grown as a driver, but he had not yet learned that the objective is to beat all the other drivers.

Jimmy never mentioned his second race at Bakersfield, where he introduced his machine to some hay bales lining the course — which meant he was going through a turn too quickly and losing control. I also learned, after the fact, that at his third race, Santa Barbara, Jimmy sent a valve through the manifold, which meant he wasn't watching his tachometer and his revs, or engine revolutions. It also meant that the engine was finished, and had to be taken apart and repaired.

Later, when I was racing and refining my natural ability, I realized that my approach to driving and to the machinery was different than Jimmy's, beginning from our racing infancy. Jimmy and I only went to one race weekend together — my first race.

Giant had completed the location shooting in Texas, and the production was moved back onto the studio sound stages. During the long absence from April to June 1955, because of the location shooting, I think Jimmy realized how much he valued and enjoyed our friendship. Even though the picture was lagging behind its shooting schedule, Jimmy himself had most nights off, and consequently we were spending a lot of time together. (On the day after Jimmy died *Giant* was still 34 days behind schedule.)

In the month that I owned the Porsche before Jimmy came back from Texas, I was out every night driving the car and testing my own handling of it along the many canyon streets off Mulholland Drive. Mulholland runs along the top of the Hollywood Hills from Cahuenga Pass, which now has the Hollywood Freeway running through it, all the way to Point Mugu. I drove the entire length of Mulholland one afternoon. I would go through the canyons, or speed along Mulholland and come back on the PCH (Pacific Coast Highway) and through a canyon to home. Dick Davalos accompanied me on one of these jaunts. He totally enjoyed it.

I have written that I loved cars and, as it turned out, my confidence in my driving was eventually substantiated by my success on the track. Somehow, I never doubted that I could race cars as well or better than anyone. I was always pretty damn good with anything having to do with hand-to-eye coordination: tennis, basketball, and ping pong, as examples. And when you get down to it, the art of race driving — and it is an art in my opinion — had everything to do with hand-to-eye coordination. Especially on sports car racing courses, which aren't oval tracks but are like real roads.

Jimmy, in my view, always looked like he belonged in a Porsche or, in fact, anything with four wheels. As if he were a part of the car. I have no idea, except for some racing pictures, how I looked in a car. But I do know how Jimmy looked to me — and he looked like he belonged there.

Jimmy and I were both lousy passengers. We needed to be behind the wheel, not just because we enjoyed driving but because we didn't trust anybody but ourselves. Having said that, both Jimmy and I trusted each other's driving and could relax in the passenger seat with the other at the wheel. Jimmy always used to say that street driving was far more dangerous than race driving because everyone on the track was going in the same direction and were, for the most part, much better drivers than the average street driver.

"The most dangerous part of a race weekend is driving to and from the track." Jimmy told me this as soon as I expressed an interest in racing, and I heard him tell other people. Jimmy absolutely believed this ... and he was right.

Now that each of us owned a Porsche, the instances of our being a passenger were few and far between, except when Jimmy, Ursula, and I were out together and we utilized Jimmy's new Ford Country Squire station wagon, a top-of-the-line model, all white with tan leather interior. Many a night found Jimmy and me in our Porsches up on Mulholland Drive taking the curves and going abreast on the two lane road that wound like a snake. There was very little traffic on Mulholland at night in those days, but still it wasn't the smartest thing to do. Of course, in our young twenties we thought we were invulnerable.

We were not reckless crazies though, by any means. We were not "pushing the edge of the envelope" up there on Mulholland. But we were competitive and had great confidence in our talent to drive at speed and control the car. I think we were both harboring secret thoughts about future confrontations in sanctioned road races under the auspices of the California Sports Car Club or the national Sports Car Club of America, commonly referred to as the CSCC and the SCCA. These night sessions didn't fully prepare me for my first race, but they did help me learn much more about the Porsche and what I could do with it. And Jimmy, who had raced three times, would tell me about what he learned on the track and what he found could be done with the car.

Mulholland did not have "view sites," although the view on a clear night was marvelous. There were places where on one side

Jimmy & Me

you could see the entire San Fernando Valley. On the other, you could see L.A. all the way to Long Beach and along the Pacific coast with a carpet of lights in both directions. Mulholland did have some dirt shoulders here and there where a motorist could pull off and park if need be. Sometimes, after driving, we would pull off, get out of the cars, and just lean against the doors. Jimmy would pull out a cigarette and light up. I didn't smoke. We would talk about the cars, racing, and whatever was going on in our lives. Sometimes we just looked down on the Valley in silence. We were very comfortable with silence. Then, depending on the thought, one of us would say something and we would discuss it.

It was on one of these stops in early September that Jimmy informed me that he wanted me to become his producer when he started to make his own films and why. We were just driving along; it was mid-afternoon and we didn't have a destination, but had just turned east off of Laurel Canyon onto Mulholland. We weren't discussing anything in particular, except Jane Deacy's forthcoming visit to deal with Warner Brothers and Jimmy's new contract. "You're going to produce all of my films," Jimmy announced, out of nowhere. Not a question; a statement. "I don't know anything about producing." I said. I wasn't exactly jumping at the chance. "You'll learn. You have to do this, you're the only one I trust, and you're good at the business stuff. I don't want anything to do with the production hassles. I want to make films." Jimmy seemed to be pleading his case. "And I don't want a studio producer anywhere near our film." I definitely caught the "our film" reference. He added, "I've already talked to Jane Deacy and told her that it has to be in the contract, and she agrees." Jimmy knew the contract was going to get done because Jane told him that Jack Warner wasn't about to let him slip away to another studio. While this was a bolt from the blue for me, it was obvious that Jimmy had been thinking about it and talking to Jane. We both let the subject drop there, for the time being. I think Jimmy knew I wasn't going to say no, and I wouldn't have.

It was during another of these Mulholland Drive conversations that we talked about how, now that I was going to race, racing numbers were important ... at least to me. Jimmy and I discussed the fact that we both wanted to thumb our noses at superstition and drive with the number 13, although both the California Sports Car Club and the Sports Car Club of America wouldn't shed their superstitions. They simply would not issue #13 to anyone. So Jimmy finally settled for #130 and I grabbed #113. We did the best we could to get number thirteen on our cars once our driver probationary periods were over. These were strategic conversations. The way both Jimmy and I looked at it, if you are going to race, you want a permanent number that you can make famous. So our numbers received as much of our attention and interest as our cars. It is the same in all sports. Athletes make their numbers famous, and this is where we were coming from.

I suppose it is somewhat ironic that about fifty years later, a German TV crew came to Hollywood to do a documentary on Jimmy for German TV and, as part of that piece, they not only interviewed me on camera, but asked me to do some driving on Mulholland. They had been provided with the latest Porsche Carrera by the Porsche distributor, and closed off Mulholland from Laurel Canyon on the east to Coldwater Canyon on the west, to film me taking the curves at speed and in four-wheel drifts. I was only about 76 at the time and enjoying every minute of it. I took a couple of dry runs in order to familiarize myself with the car, and to learn where the cameras would be placed. After a few minutes I felt right at home in the car. I hadn't driven a Porsche in twenty years, but aside from being faster, I felt it handled the same as ever. They had placed cameras at two different locations, but they also put a camerawoman and a camera in the small space behind the seats so that they could shoot my hands on the wheel and the side of my face as I drove at speed. After two runs, the camerawoman had to get out — she got sick!

I got a call from the producer of this documentary about three days later telling me that the shots were great, and that the crew was awed by the fact that the film taken with the on-board camera showed my hands being rock steady, and my facial expression never changing from complete concentration with an absence of any emotion. I never really had thought about it, but after he told me, I realized that was what I hoped I was like behind the wheel.

Getting back to 1955, Jimmy and Ursula were a twosome at this time and, unless they were going to an "invitation-only" party or some studio function that Jimmy had to attend, they insisted we make it a threesome whenever we got together. These were mainly movie and coffee occasions, and Jimmy's new Ford Country Squire Station Wagon came in very handy. Jimmy had a horse on a ranch, so why not a Country Squire with wood paneling on the sides? Jimmy and Ursula always made me feel like we were a threesome on these outings, and never did I feel it was a twosome plus one.

Ursula Andress had a very pretty face, naturally. She never wore much in the way of makeup, if any, but she was simply a pretty woman. Even when she came up to the pool with no makeup or hairdo, just in her bathing suit, she was pretty — she didn't need any help.

This leads me to a little story: Jimmy wanted out of his garage apartment. He needed more room and more privacy. One night at the Villa Capri, Jimmy and Nikko Romanos began conversing about Jimmy's predicament. Nikko told us that he owned a sort of chalet-type place in Sherman Oaks, which was about ten minutes down Ventura Boulevard from our house and a great location for Jimmy at the time. Nikko's chalet or lodge had a large front room with a sliding glass door across part of the front, and a driveway to the left of the front door. A bed-loft faced you as you entered, with a kitchen at the far end. To the right of the kitchen was a stairway to a kind of basement den. The place had a small enclosed front yard with grass and a few trees. It was a hunting lodge, San Fernando Valley style, and was only fifteen minutes or less straight down Ventura towards Hollywood to Warner Brothers. It was next door to Van Nuys Boulevard, which leads to Mulholland and access to four canyons leading to L.A., Hollywood, and Beverly Hills. Jimmy could finally invite guests like Liz Taylor over to his place.

Jimmy moved in, and we were now able to go down to the den or sit at the kitchen table talking about things, deep philosophical conversations like, "Is it possible to have sex in a Porsche?" This was a subject of great interest and importance to us. After all, one would have to overcome the problem of the two bucket seats, and I don't mean today's seats. These were not leather and had little or no padding. They were true bucket seats. And then there was the lack of space and the steering wheel. And not only no back seat, but between the bucket seats sat a handle like the handle on an outside water faucet that turned the heat on and off. I mean — this was an engineering equation that we were trying to solve.

A few days after this conversation took place, I came home about 10:30 p.m. and found my mother up, and waiting for me, which was unusual. I thought something had happened in the family, but she only wanted to tell me that Jimmy had dropped by about an hour before with a girl in the car. I asked who she was. My mom said she didn't know because neither she nor Jimmy got out of the car, and all she could see was the dark hair.

Jimmy & Me

My mom asked Jimmy if he wanted to leave a message for me, and Jimmy said, "Just tell Lew that the answer is yes!"

My mom didn't have any idea what he was talking about. "Is that all?" she asked, and Jimmy replied, "Yep!" and drove off. Of course I knew exactly what Jimmy was talking about. The next night, when I saw Jimmy, he told me that the girl in the car was Natalie Wood. The reader should understand that, in our technical discussions about this gymnastic feat, outside the car didn't count, although Jimmy turned that trick in Palm Springs. I thought it would take two contortionists to do the deed, but Jimmy was more optimistic. And being Jimmy, he had to prove or disprove it as soon as possible.

Talk about "The cat that ate the canary!" Let's face it, Jimmy didn't climb Mt. Everest, or discover uranium with this one, but he sure as hell was proud of this prodigious accomplishment. I did point out that he only got half the credit. Not only did Natalie participate, but I made the point that, in my humble opinion, she had the tougher job. Jimmy laughed so hard I thought he would lose his front teeth.

July, and the summer of '55 had begun. To be more precise, this period actually covered July through September, but in my mind it will always be the summer of '55, Jimmy's last summer. Jimmy had moved to Nikko's place at 14611 Sutton Street, a block or two west of Ventura Boulevard.

Jimmy bought his station wagon shortly after he moved. He had rented a U-Haul type of vehicle to move with, and I think that is when he realized he needed to have something larger than a Porsche. July also saw Jimmy, Ursula and me going to see "flicks" as a threesome. I recall one night in particular going down to Wilshire Boulevard near Highland, just two blocks from where I used to live and go to school, to the 4-Star Theater to see Julie Harris in *I Am a Camera*. This was the movie based on the play that later became the musical *Cabaret*. After the movie we ended up at the Hamburger Hamlet, sitting on the small terrace outside and watching the Strip traffic go by.

Ursula and Jimmy discussed the movie and the performances. Jimmy liked the film and Julie Harris' performance. Jimmy of course played opposite Julie in *Eden*, and thought of her as a very talented actress. He talked about the fact that her character in the film was not only the central character, but the entire film revolves around her, and how well she carried that off. Ursula liked both the film and Julie, but did more listening to Jimmy than talking. She would agree here and there — but was more like an acting student listening to the teacher.

We went to other movies, but *Camera* was the only current release that we ever went to see. Older movies that Jimmy had reasons to want to see were our targets, and Jimmy would give me some insight by actually discussing them. One night, after viewing the John Ford film *Fort Apache*, he turned to me and said, "John Ford can make *The Grapes of Wrath* and *Fort Apache*. What other director can do that?" I actually had more titles in my head than Jimmy, and I suggested we find and see noir films like *The Glass Key* and *This Gun for Hire*, two Alan Ladd early films that made him a star. Jimmy loved them. He told me, "Ladd is a little wooden (a term he used to describe Massey in *Eden*), but he has a screen presence and he was born for film noir." Jimmy talked more about the directors involved in these two film noir classics. He really liked the camera work and lighting in film noir, and said, "These films wouldn't be special if they had used Technicolor." He thought the lighting directors should have gotten much more credit, and that a director could say a lot more in black and white than one could in color. "Some actresses are just born for film noir," he told me once after seeing Liz Scott in a film. "Who else?" I asked, because I had my own favorites. "Bacall, Jane Greer, the Columbia lot has a few." Jimmy said. This may be the only time Jimmy and I discussed acting on any level.

On a point of interest, this was the age of the serious dramatic Broadway actor coming out to Hollywood to do a movie: The age of "method acting," of the Actor's Studio, of realism and high drama. Of Marlon Brando's *Streetcar Named Desire*, Ben Gazzara's *A Hatful of Rain*, and Rod Steiger's *The Pawnbroker*. And now Jimmy coming onto the scene in *Eden* and *Rebel*. Yet, Jimmy wanted to seek out the comedies, from madcap films like *Topper* and *The Awful Truth*, to *My Favorite Wife* and *Ninotchka*. Jimmy really had making a comedy as one of his top priorities.

Jimmy considered Preston Sturges a genius of film comedy, and we searched out *The Miracle of Morgan's Creek*, *The Palm Beach Story*, *Sullivan's Travels*, and others. Ernst Lubitsch was another director that Jimmy "studied," and he worshiped at the altar of Orson Welles' *Citizen Kane*. Camera angles, light and shadows, unknown great talent, and going where no one had gone before fascinated Jimmy. There was no doubt in my mind that when he could direct and pick his own material, Jimmy would make a western and a comedy, and perhaps a film in black and white. Above all else, Jimmy wanted the freedom to make his own films.

Chapter Twelve

SUMMERTIME ... AND STORMY WEATHER

In Los Angeles, during the months of July and August, you can count on warm weather and hot weather in the San Fernando Valley, and the summer of 1955 was no exception. That year there were also some dark clouds that had nothing to do with the weather.

Jimmy and I were spending the most time we had ever spent together, and that led to many conversations; some serious about the future and others simply entertaining young-guy talk. These conversations took place wherever we happened to be: my house, Jimmy's place, the Villa and, as you know, on top of Mulholland by our parked cars. As the days passed, some of these conversations became grimmer, more serious, and accompanied by stress on Jimmy's part, because of problems that unfolded on the *Giant* set between him and George Stevens.

My first visit to the set of *Giant* was preceded by the usual lunch in the Green Room, but the visit stopped being usual when Jimmy showed me his new Ford Country Squire station wagon. It became even more unusual when we got into the wagon and proceeded to drive slowly to the sound stage.

As we drove, we came upon Liz Taylor in full antebellum dress, hoop skirt and all, walking to the sound stage. Jimmy stopped and asked, "Want a lift?" Liz gave us a big smile and said, "Great." I hopped out to get in back because Jimmy had the back seat down flat in hauling mode, but Liz wouldn't hear of it. She climbed in the back, and sat cross-legged on the flat surface.

Jimmy & Me

"Are you okay?" Jimmy asked and Liz replied, "I'm just fine." Jimmy introduced us, and Liz gave me a smile and said, "So you're Lew." Not a question, a statement. I answered, "Yes, I'm afraid so." Obviously Jimmy had talked to Liz about me. I found Liz to be gracious, unassuming, and very friendly.

The water was beginning to boil in July, and after shooting was completed on a Friday night, one or both of the assistant directors were sent by George Stevens to tell Jimmy to be on the set at 8:00 a.m. the following morning. This instruction came after Stevens had purposely, and probably with malice aforethought, ordered Jimmy on the set at 8:00 a.m. that morning, and let him sit around all day without ever using him. To me, this was simply a juvenile power play that was prevalent in Hollywood in the studio days as a way to discipline actors and let them know who was boss.

I know that in Jimmy's opinion, this was where he drew the line in the sand. The *Giant* set had constantly been a troubled set, insofar as George Stevens and Jimmy were concerned. And of course, Jimmy was getting no support from Jack Warner or from his "hatchet" man Steve Trilling. To Jack Warner, who was still living in the days of the old Hollywood studio system, actors could be suspended at no risk. Stevens was known for his penchant for tight control over his actors, for his constant retakes, and for his way of reprimanding actors who challenged him. And Jimmy did challenge Stevens plenty in Texas, and was continuing to do so on the sound stage.

As I got it from Jimmy (the first and rare time he discussed anything with me that was going on acting-wise), the trouble developed from Stevens' insistence that Jimmy play a scene his way, and Jimmy seeing the character differently. A lot of problems could have been avoided if George Stevens had been more diplomatic and less interested in being the winner. Stevens was a great director who made some memorable films, but he too was living in the old studio dictatorial system, and transition was already happening. They all failed to realize that there had never been a James Dean before — and you cannot put a bridle on a shooting star. Jimmy wasn't into playing games or power plays. He was all about the project and his character. This was the same weekend that Jimmy had planned to move from his garage apartment to Nikko's chalet in Sherman Oaks. Jimmy soon turned Stevens' machinations into a question of "Where's Jimmy?" Whether Stevens was actually going to shoot some of Jimmy's scenes that next morning or not didn't signify. Jimmy never showed up. Stevens' tactic backfired and led to a climactic ending. Eight a.m. Saturday morning, July 26, came and no Jimmy. Soon a call went out to Dick Clayton. Where was Jimmy? The lot was searched to see if he was on the premises, but to no avail. Again, more calls to Dick Clayton; these were more panicky. The production was already well behind schedule and above budget and, according to Stevens, Jimmy was going to be used extensively Saturday. No one knew where Jimmy was, except for the Bracker family ...

Liz Taylor was once quoted publicly making this observation about Jimmy: "He was very afraid of being hurt. He was afraid of opening up in case it was turned around against him." Liz had that right, generally speaking — but I wonder if she ever knew what I actually witnessed — Jimmy opening up to me and my family during the summer of 1955.

By the end of July, Jimmy had become a part of our household. He would drop in unannounced, coming and going as he pleased. He didn't need an invitation, and felt very comfortable simply being around or not. He was totally at ease with my mom and dad, and chatted with them all the time. He would even raid the refrigerator, which was always full, because my mother was always cooking and baking. And Jimmy was like my dad —

Jimmy & Me

he loved coffee — and my mother's home-baked Jewish coffee cakes.

On weekends, Jimmy would be up at the house listening to my record collection and hanging around the pool. A later generation would call it "hanging out." My collection included jazz groups, opera, big band jazz, and Broadway. We had speakers around the patio, so we didn't have to be inside.

Jimmy would also bring Ursula, but not all the time. In fact, Ursula sometimes came up during the day at weekends unannounced, whether Jimmy was there or not. She felt comfortable just lying around the pool. Usually she brought a girlfriend, the French actress/dancer Josiane (Josey) Berenger, who was her roommate, and who at the time was purportedly engaged to Marlon Brando.

But this particular Saturday morning had a special purpose. Jimmy did not go into specifics, but he said he had to get away from the studio for a while and on the off-chance that somebody would call for him, he asked my folks and me to say we hadn't seen him. I knew what it was all about, and my folks understood this was Jimmy's business. No one at the studio knew me or my telephone numbers. In fact, the phones were in my dad's name, although I wasn't certain whether or not Jimmy had given Dick Clayton my phone numbers. Evidently he didn't, because Dick never called, though Jimmy did talk to him from our house.

I was acutely aware that the studio was looking for Jimmy, as were my parents. I learned later that everyone was really frantic. The Warner people, and I mean Jack Warner's top attack dog, Steve Trilling, were burning up the lines to Dick Clayton. They even called Jane Deacy in New York. I believed then, and still do today, that Jimmy had advised Jane what he was doing. He had complete trust in Jane, and would have talked it over with her beforehand. And Jane Deacy was one smart agent. *Rebel* was "in the can," and she had already assessed Jimmy's growing power in Hollywood and knew how far she could push Warner Brothers and George Stevens. Actually, she was already having more than preliminary conversations with Jack Warner on a new and much more lucrative and powerful contract for Jimmy.

As for Jimmy, he was lolling around the pool, or sitting on the patio talking to my dad or whatever visitors were there. We always had visitors. But Jimmy seemed pretty relaxed now that he had made this move. He was talkative and in good humor — I might even say he was enjoying it. Jimmy didn't really talk about it that weekend, except when he was on the phone with Dick Clayton, but he did mention it in a laughing manner: "What can they do, suspend me? Nope, they're behind schedule now, and I know Jack (Warner) wants this new contract badly." So he did talk with Jane.

When Jimmy was ready, some time on Saturday, he finally called Dick Clayton and told him what the problem was, and that he wasn't returning to work until it was settled. He swore Dick to secrecy as to his whereabouts. Everything went through Dick to the studio. Our house was the command post, and Jimmy was the commanding general. Dick would call the house and leave a message, and Jimmy would call Dick back when he was ready. But Dick was under instructions from Jimmy, and I presume Jane Deacy, that Jimmy's location was not to be revealed.

A meeting was eventually set up in Steve Trilling's office for the following Monday, and a working agreement was to be hashed out between Jimmy and Stevens. One might call it an "armed truce," but at least the film would get finished. Until that happened, even my mom and dad were briefed by Jimmy, and they screened any calls having to do with him — it was a family conspiracy!

Although Jimmy had artistic problems with George Stevens on *Giant*, let's not forget that Stevens was a master filmmaker, a Hollywood Icon and a great judge of talent. My old friend Dan Tana, sometime after the Villa Capri era, became involved in film production, and became a friend of George Stevens. One day, they were talking about James Dean. Dan related this story to me recently, when he and I were both filming interviews for a new film, *Post Modern Conclusions on the Death of James Dean*. According to Dan, Stevens acknowledged to him, "Hollywood does not realize what they have lost. The loss of James Dean is the biggest loss in Hollywood history."

As I got it from Jimmy, there was to be no more game-playing and much more collaboration and freedom as to how Jimmy's character was to be portrayed. I have always felt that the central problem was that the studio was as uncomfortable as I was with Jimmy portraying an aging character, and their inability to fully commit to that happening in the film. Jimmy was going to portray an older man after two films as a young icon. I felt it was much too early in his career — I think they were very nervous about it also.

Giant has always been my least favorite of Jimmy's three movies. I know that it was the least favorite of Jimmy's to work on, and that included his performance on the sound stage portion of the film. Jimmy was very fond of Liz Taylor and his time with the wranglers and stunt men in Texas, but he wasn't fond of much else about the *Giant* experience. He felt pretty good about his performance in the first part of the film, but not the second half where he ages.

Lew Bracker

Outside of the *Giant* saga, the days at the pool were great. They were totally un-Hollywood, relaxed and really pretty normal. Jimmy would do whatever he wanted to around the house and so would I. I wasn't the host and Jimmy wasn't the guest. We weren't attached at the hip. Jimmy might be doing one thing in one room, usually mine, while I would be doing something else outside, or watching TV. One weekend my dad's sister Lil was visiting us from Nogales. I happened to glance over, and there was Jimmy sitting on the patio talking to her. Knowing Jimmy, he was probably asking all kinds of questions about Nogales and how the family found their way there from Brooklyn, N.Y.

On another occasion I noticed Jimmy and my dad sitting off in a corner of the patio in deep conversation. I didn't venture over when I saw Jimmy talking one-on-one with someone up at the house, whether it was my dad, or anyone else. I knew Jimmy, and I knew very well what it was all about. This was Jimmy's "thing," and not my business. Dad, as a 20-year-old, went down to the building of the Panama Canal and was Secretary to the Commanding General. My Uncle Charlie, Adele Rosenman's father, was also down there in an administrative capacity, and Charlie and Joe shared a rented house. It wasn't long before they sent for my Aunt Lil, age 17, to come down from Brooklyn and keep house for them. That story, plus how she and her brothers ended up in Nogales, was fodder for Jimmy's curiosity.

Added to those adventures, my dad, after Panama, worked for Shell Oil in the rough early days in Mexico before joining Charlie, who had opened an Army and Navy war surplus store in Nogales, selling World War 1 surplus to the revolutionary fighters in Mexico. Charlie stayed in Nogales and ran the store, while my father (who could speak, write and type Spanish like a native) went into Mexico to sell guns and stuff to people like Zapata and others fighting under Benito Juarez. These stories of my dad's were fields of clover for Jimmy's insatiable curiosity.

Jimmy & Me

Jimmy was very content to be there around the pool with my family. My mother, to paraphrase Gilbert & Sullivan, was the very model of the proverbial Jewish mother. She was always bringing out food and, of course, insisting that Jimmy eat. But there were instances when we would just hop in one of the cars, clad only in bathing trunks, and shoot a few blocks down to the Boulevard, as Ventura was called, to one of our favorite places on the corner of Ventura and Coldwater Canyon, The Hot Dog Show.

This place grilled their dogs, and their menu consisted of dogs of all kinds. For instance, the "Dachshund" had sauerkraut on it, and the "Boston Bull" contained baked beans. Well, you get the idea. We would load up on this stuff and bring it back to the house for Ursula and whoever else was up there. Almost every Sunday, my dad had his old pinochle friends up there playing cards on the patio. One of them, Dr. Irving Berman, became Jimmy's doctor, and signed his medical certificate for his racing license.

From the early '40s through the '80s I always owned at least one Labrador retriever as a friend and companion. The first one was named Michelina. The Labrador I got as a weaned puppy in Santa Barbara upon getting out of the Army I named Michelina II, for though I had quite a few Labs in between, I never forgot my first Michelina. I owned Amber and Farina who were out of Michelina's first litter.

Michelina, or "Mick" or "Mickey" as I called her, loved the water and loved to retrieve almost anything. If I threw a ball into the pool, Michelina would go flying through the air off the side into the pool to retrieve it. If no one was playing with her and it was really hot — the valley side of the Hollywood Hills was at least 10 degrees warmer than the L.A. side — Mickey would go lay down on the top step of the pool and just cool off. But she would not go off the board! Only off the side. She would get on the board but she would not step off, much less fly off. If you got her up on the board, which was easy, and then threw a ball into the pool, she would look at it and then dash around to the side and leap in.

This was a challenge to Jimmy. Jimmy tried all of that August to get Mick to go off the board after a ball. He would get her up on the board and talk to her. He would show her the ball and merely drop it into the water. Mickey would look at the ball and run off the board to the side of the pool and dive in. Jimmy tried walking out to the end of the board with a ball and getting Michelina to get on the board. He would try to coax her out to where he was, even passionately drawing out her name "M-i-c-h-e-l-i-n-a." Mick would just look at him and then run around to the side of the pool waiting for him to drop the ball. Jimmy tried hard, but Michelina prevailed. And to the end of her life, she shunned the board and dived off the edge of the pool.

In August, Ursula became noticeable by her absence. She stopped coming to the house. I was to learn that John Derek had entered the picture and wanted to marry her, and did. I said earlier that Jimmy had only the one love in his life and that was Pier. I can also say, because I was there, that Jimmy really didn't miss too much of a beat when Ursula switched to John Derek. He wasn't even out of sorts and certainly not heartbroken. I think Jimmy knew that a split would happen sooner or later. As I look back, Jimmy never even mentioned Ursula to me after that. It was like a seamless change. Of course I knew; but as always, I let Jimmy tell me what he wanted to tell me.

Having said that, I recall an incident, and I remember that I was very much aware of it at the time: my bedroom was on the opposite side of the house from my folks and it had a sliding glass door to the patio, an access I used all the time. This one

Jimmy & Me

time I came inside my bedroom to change records on the turntable changer, and came upon Ursula and Jimmy "necking." They broke apart like teenagers and both were definitely a little embarrassed, as if they shouldn't do that in front of me.

After his split from Ursula, Jimmy started dating again, and one weekend he brought up a starlet from Universal who had made some films for them, a young lady by the name of Lori Nelson. I don't know who put them together, and I know this was their first date. But Lori was very "girlish," so sweet and vanilla, and not what Jimmy was interested in. She was all over Jimmy, oohing and cooing and telling him about her doll collection, her cutesy bedroom with dolls on the bed and all over the room. This kind of conversation made Jimmy cringe. Jimmy never saw her again.

I don't know if it was because we knew each other so well now, or because we were much closer, but Jimmy and I had a couple of conversations regarding the making of a movie or movies. These also took place at our pool. They were casual and very entertaining. But as I look back on them now I wonder if there was a serious undertone — that they really would have happened had Jimmy lived.

We were talking casually about movies, and somehow the conversation went to, "Why not make an anti-Western?" This was in 1955 when TV was full of Western series, and many movie Westerns were still being produced. But no one would have dared, had they thought of it, to make an "anti-Western." This was also two decades before *Blazing Saddles*.

As we got into it, we were laughing over every suggested piece of "business." At one point we were laughing so hard that my mother, who couldn't tell a joke because she would start laughing so hard she couldn't finish it, came out to see what we were laughing about. We had started with the concept of a parody or take-off on the standard Western with all its clichés. It had nothing to do with race or *Blazing Saddles*. After all, this was 1955 and a decade before Selma and Montgomery, Alabama.

All through film history the Westerns were made to a strict formula, the great American morality play, and no one had thought of or dared make a Western parody. So here we were vocally throwing in all the shticks we could think of: a guy jumping from the balcony onto his horse, but missing the horse, and the brave Indian fighter meeting with the Great Chief and speaking in sign language, with the Chief answering in Oxfordian-English that he hasn't the faintest idea what those signs mean. We had the "hero" make the rear of the horse leap into the saddle but vault over the horse's head. We had a great time this one afternoon vocalizing our Western screenplay.

Another sunny afternoon at the pool (and this may dismay some people in Jimmy's background), we engaged in the same kind of parody, this time having to do with a Biblical movie. Hollywood certainly had made its share of religious epics over the years. But none like ours. We had Mary having an affair with Joseph and, after getting her pregnant and visibly so, Joseph and Mary decided to hit the road because no one in their neighborhood would buy such a cockamamie story as an immaculate conception. However, Joseph felt that in a big city like Bethlehem there were still a lot of superstitious people and besides, they could lose themselves in the crowds.

As we envisioned our epic, Mary and Joseph's immediate problem was transportation. Mary refused to schlep to Bethlehem, wherever that was, on the back of a donkey. Joseph told her to get her ass on the ass or stay and get stoned ... literally. So off they went. At first their plan was simple. Claim a

Jimmy & Me

miracle and live quietly ever after. But on the journey, Joseph started to think about it, once he tuned out Mary's kvetching, and he began to flesh out a new idea. He came to the conclusion that, "From this a mensch could make a living! I mean look at Moses and what he did with the burning bush story, and that slab of stone with the ten scratchings on it. I'm broke and can't pay for a room. Besides, the town has been over-booked for weeks. I'll find a barn, have the baby, surround him with a few pigs and goats, and get three guys from Central Casting and costumes from *Road to Morocco* and we're in business."

As shocking as this might have been to some, we just kept the ideas rolling, and laughed about seeing Cecil B. DeMille's face if such a picture were ever made.

The months of July and August were bittersweet. Most of the time the living was easy, but the problems in July and August on *Giant* had Jimmy stressed a lot of the time. Yet, in retrospect, our house was a real escape from everything for Jimmy Dean, and I mean that in both senses. He escaped from his troubles at Warner, and it was a vacation escape at the same time. Jimmy appeared to not have a care in the world when up at our house. He was smiling, laughing and in conversation with a member of my family or whoever was up there — and there were always people up there. Our house was an open house that the family called "Shirley's half-way house," because it was always halfway to wherever you were going to or coming from and they always stopped in. Jimmy loved it.

Chapter Thirteen

"THE BIG SNEAK"

The night of September 1, 1955, was a memorable night for two very different reasons — and the events of that night must have their own chapter.

I was at work in the office when Jimmy called me in the middle of the afternoon and asked me to meet him at the Villa Capri around 5:30 p.m. He also mentioned that it was important, in the event I might have other plans. He went on to say that we would have a bite to eat and would be gone all evening. Well, Jimmy didn't have to tell me all that because just meeting him at the Villa at the unheard of hour of 5:30 p.m. raised a red flag — and certainly piqued my curiosity.

It was a common practice for the major studios to "sneak" preview a film for live theater-going audiences so that they, the studios, could measure audience reaction to the movie and its stars. The studios would pick an outlying theater, even as far away as Santa Barbara. Sneaks differed from premières in that the theater would advertise "an important major film preview" and that was all. No title, no stars. The theater would then show their main attraction around 6:00 p.m. followed by the sneak preview at around 7:30 p.m. to 8:00 p.m.

I had been to many sneak previews before, just as a movie goer. In our teens we used to peruse the movie section of the *Times* to seek them out. And we learned early on that if we took a look at the *Hollywood Reporter* or *Variety*, many times you could figure out what was being previewed.

Jimmy & Me

When I got to the Villa for the earliest meal we were ever to have there, I found that Dick Clayton was joining us, and that he was driving us to a movie house in Huntington Park where Warner was sneaking *Rebel Without a Cause*. And that is what we did. We had dinner, and then Dick drove us in his new Ford convertible to Huntington Park, a suburb of L.A. (isn't every place?) The top was down on a warm and balmy Southern California evening. On the way, Dick talked mostly shop talk; I just sat in the back seat and listened. Seems the top Warner execs including marketing and distribution people would be at the preview. So it was an especially big deal. Not just marketing guys.

Jimmy really didn't have much to say, but Dick was enthusiastic. Dick Clayton was a very nice, gentle guy — he wasn't a sycophant or a panderer. He simply did his job and handled Jimmy — the times I was with them both — efficiently, eagerly, and unselfishly. Dick had no ego that I could discover.

We arrived at the theatre, and the regular feature was still on, so the theater manager ushered us into his office to sit and wait without people seeing Jimmy. The movie ended in about ten minutes, but we waited until the intermission was over and the house lights were dimmed for the start of the preview. The manager then ushered us to a section in the rear of the theater where Warner's people were sitting. Significantly, Jimmy was the only member of the cast in that section.

The Warner Brothers logo flashed on the screen, and the audience seemed to be anticipating something big. When Jimmy's name came up above the title, a roar of excitement went up in the theater. I have never ever, before or since, experienced anything like it at a preview. The reaction from the audience was such that I can only liken it to the night Ed Sullivan introduced the Beatles on TV. No, it was different. In my opinion the teenagers weren't just watching Jimmy, they were living what Jimmy was acting out on the screen. They were saying to themselves: "That's me. That's the way I feel!"

That wasn't the only difference. This was not just an audience of girls in their teens. This was also an audience of boys as well, and adults. I have always believed to this day that the reason Jimmy and his films have lived on all these years is because generations come and go — but basically teenagers are teenagers. Each generation of teenagers has a lot in common emotionally with all the others: the same insecurities, the same pressures, and the same angst. So each succeeding generation discovers James Dean and reacts in the same way. Jimmy is eternally young because of his films, and is discovered by every new generation of teenagers, which embraces him and becomes emotionally attached. In *Eden* and *Rebel*, Jimmy spoke for teenagers.

The audience didn't get over their excitement until most of the credits had run their course. Remember, this was September of 1955. *East of Eden* was the only James Dean film the public had seen, yet such was Jimmy's screen magnetism and appeal to teenagers and movie goers world-wide that they were actively craving another Dean film.

The audience was very quiet throughout the movie. It seemed to me they were very involved, intense, and focused on every single scene — and almost hypnotized when Jimmy was on the screen. I realized I was very aware of the audience's reaction as the movie progressed. I was actually watching them. My take on Jimmy was that I think he was studying the film itself, and not so much his own work. He wasn't fidgety and made no sign of approval or disapproval.

Jimmy & Me

As the movie was closing and "The End" appeared on the screen, we all left before the lights came up to go back to the manager's office and wait for the preview cards to be gathered up. At every preview, audience reaction cards are given out to the audience as they come out of the theater and are asked that they be filled out, answering basic questions like: "Did you like the picture?" "Did you like the stars?" "Which star did you like the most?" and on. The studio execs were a little edgy because, as we slipped out of the theater, the audience was almost silent. There was little applause, but there was a lot of murmuring going on. This worried the Warner people.

Jimmy just seemed like Jimmy. He wasn't saying much, and appeared to be appraising his performance and the finished product in his mind.

After about ten minutes or so, the manager came in with a huge pile of cards. He said, "This is an unusual amount of responses, I think every person filled out a card." The studio men each took a portion of the cards with more than a little trepidation and began to read each response. We could tell right away they were visibly stunned. They were looking at each other and then at Jimmy.

The responses, without exception, were full of praise for the movie, but that doesn't even begin to describe how they felt about Jimmy. It seemed they couldn't find praise enough for James Dean. Samples of the cards I actually read called Jimmy "sensational," "fantastic," "greatest movie experience in my life," "James Dean speaks for me," and "greatest acting I ever saw." The cards could not have been more effusive if the Warner PR department themselves had filled them out.

I sat there with Jimmy and Dick listening to the Warner people talk to each other. They couldn't contain themselves, and probably forgot that Jimmy and Dick were sitting there listening, because this wasn't going to help them when contract negotiations began later in September. Jimmy was calm and quiet on the way back to the Villa, mostly listening to Dick, who was ecstatic and very excited.

I heard he went to another sneak with Ursula later, but if he did, he had already seen the film and the reaction, so I think he did it for Ursula. It was a night to remember — and to savor. A night that always stood out in my memory, but took me a while to realize all that the night meant to both Jimmy and me.

We got back to the Villa and ended up in the same booth where we had dinner earlier. It was the first booth in the main room against the right-hand wall. I tell you this because it figures into the evening that was not yet over. Jimmy sat in his usual corner slouch facing the other booths, and I sat with my back to the other booths on that wall. Dick had said his goodbyes in the parking lot.

We weren't in the Villa more than ten minutes when Natalie, Nick Adams, and Dennis Hopper walked in. They had been at the preview, but I hadn't seen them. They were in the audience and not ushered about like we were. As fate would have it, they took the booth adjoining ours, along one wall. Natalie and Nick sat with their backs to me and Dennis across the table facing our booth. I just can't help but reflect, as I write this, that of that night's group of people: James Dean, Natalie Wood, Dennis Hopper, Nick Adams, and me – I'm the only survivor.

Natalie was particularly excited, and she draped herself over the top of the booth, and started chatting with me about the film like an old friend — what did I think, etc. I had never talked to Natalie in my life, but I told her I thought it was a very important film, and that everyone in it was going to benefit.

Jimmy & Me

Natalie was smiling, laughing, and jabbering — she was over the moon. After about five minutes of this, in a mean, if not nasty voice, Nick Adams called out, "Are you with him or with me?" Not us as in "Me and Dennis Hopper," but ME. Natalie made a face that only Jimmy and I could see, raising her eyebrows. She made a silent "ooh" with her mouth and said, "I better go back."

When I turned back to Jimmy, who had silently watched this little episode, he had his familiar half-smile, half-smirk on his face. He did not say a word about this, not then and not later, but his expression was one of "I know what that was all about." I just turned back to Jimmy with a kind of smile that I hoped conveyed my message: "He's got a real problem."

Jimmy and I went back to talking about other things, and he never said a word to the other booth all evening. Nick was struggling with two insecurities that night, only one of which I was previously aware. I knew, of course, about his problem with Jimmy, but I didn't know that Nick also thought that he and Natalie were going together. And so, not only did Nick resent me because of Jimmy, but he was also now fuming in the Villa booth because Natalie was half out of their booth and half-way into my side of our booth carrying on an animated conversation — with me of all people. Natalie and I had never really met — but being a product of Hollywood, even at the age of seventeen — she would have made a definite note of me with Jimmy on the *Rebel* set, and wasn't bothering with an introduction.

I realize that as we got into September, celebrity was something we had to deal with in our friendship — and, more to the point, in Jimmy's life. But we never talked about it except in the same terms as you would with any rising, successful young man. Yes, we had plans for a restaurant and a Porsche dealership — that was fun talk. But we talked about a will, life insurance, and estate planning because we knew — in general if not in particular — that Jimmy was going to be making quite a bit more money very soon. I explained to him that, as a celebrity, he was now what the insurance companies considered a "target risk" and he had to get protected and organized. Later in 1955, I was able to put Jimmy with a leading entertainment business management firm that would pay all his bills and take care of his business details. Jimmy loved it. But we had to go slowly. Even with 1950 dollars, Jimmy only got $9,000 for *Rebel* and $21,000 for *Giant*. But he did not have money to burn at present, and so my actions were dictated by what Jimmy could afford. An accident policy was actually the least costly, and so that is where I started.

East of Eden was now in the theaters and *Rebel* was to begin shooting in March, so Jimmy had some time available for us to get some of his business in order. To this end, I was in Jimmy's dressing room on the Warner lot on 20 February 1955, for the express purpose of getting an application filled out for a $100,000 accident policy. That was a lot of money in those days. Jimmy was shaving while I got his answers to the application's questions and filled them in. When I arrived at the Beneficiary question, Jimmy said, "Put in your name and we can deal with it later." I said, "Jimmy, I won't do that," and he replied, "I don't know; I'll tell you later." I told Jimmy that until he had a will we could just put down "estate," and take care of the will when he had the time. Jimmy was happy to get rid of the responsibility in that manner, and neither one of us gave it another thought. After *Rebel*, Jimmy would have loads of time.

Chapter Fourteen

OFF TO THE RACES!

In early August, the idea of my joining the sports car racing organizations and actually racing my Porsche moved from my subconscious to a very conscious thought. It then became an imperative action. I must have known, deep inside, that I was buying the Porsche to race it.

I began making some off-hand remarks about the idea to Jimmy in July, some weeks before the Santa Barbara Road Races slated for September 3-4. Predictably, Jimmy seized on the idea. In fact, he was super enthusiastic, but was careful not to push me. Jimmy also planned to put in his entry form in the hope that *Giant* would be finished and he would no longer be prohibited by Warner Brothers from racing. Jimmy still had his Porsche speedster at this point in time, and somehow it didn't occur to us that we would be driving against each other. At least, it didn't occur to me, and Jimmy didn't mention it. I knew so little about how things worked that I probably assumed there was a novice race. There wasn't. I was just excited now that I had made my decision.

On an August afternoon, I went down to the California Sports Car Club offices in Hollywood, and picked up the necessary forms and filled them out in order to be able to participate as a probationary driver. One of the requirements was a medical certificate from my doctor. For some reason, Jimmy needed to take care of this piece of business also, even though he had already raced in three races. It never occurred to me to ask Jimmy how he was cleared to race if he hadn't a medical clearance on file. I got mine from our family doctor and long-time friend of my dad, Irving Berman. Jimmy, plagued by *Giant* being so far behind schedule, did not get his from Dr. Berman until September 24, for the Salinas races.

It was after Jimmy knew for a fact that *Giant* would not be finished in time for him to race at Santa Barbara, and I was officially entered, that it dawned on me that I would not have the added distraction and pressure in my first race of driving against Jimmy. It really was the perfect time to make my debut.

I did not mention any of my racing plans to my folks. I was operating under the theory that what they don't know won't hurt them (or worry them). As for me, fear never entered the picture then or ever over my entire driving career. I hardly ever mentioned what I was doing with my personal life except if I was getting interested in some girl, and my parents never asked except for my mother trying to fix me up with someone's daughter. I didn't clue Jimmy into my parents not knowing, because the subject never came up between us. Of course, my folks knowing or not wouldn't have occurred to Jimmy. He had been on his own without answering to anybody for years. My folks found out the last week of August, and the messenger was Jimmy.

Jimmy had told me earlier that he was giving me his helmet for luck in my racing career. I smiled and said "Thanks." My first thought was that I wouldn't have to go out and buy one. I didn't even know where to get one. I know now that this gift of Jimmy's own helmet was a gesture of genuine emotion and caring. It wasn't a loan; it was a gift.

It was in the week before the race on Tuesday or Wednesday that I received a strange phone call from my dad. He asked, "When do you think you'll be coming home today?" I told him

Jimmy & Me

it would be late afternoon, and he asked if I could come home an hour or so earlier. I said I would. The phone call puzzled me because it was really out of the ordinary, but I wasn't puzzled for long. Within ten minutes of hearing from my dad, I got a call from Jimmy.

It seems that in his excitement over my first race and, in what I believe, Jimmy wanting to be as much a part of the event as possible, he had run up to my house in the middle of the day with the helmet. Jimmy walked in through the kitchen side door as we all did — as I've said Jimmy was just one of the family — and right into my mother. He said, "I just came up to drop off the helmet for Lew." My mother looked at Jimmy and then at the helmet, and asked: "So why does Lew need a helmet?"

My mother told me later that Jimmy's face got red. He said: "Oops!" And then launched into a non-stop defense of his role: "I had nothing to do with it. He never told me until he had already entered the race. Really, I didn't push him." This was true. My mother told me that Jimmy then handed her the helmet, mumbled something about having to get to the studio, and beat a hasty retreat. My dad told me, laughing, "Jimmy lit out of here like his tail feathers were on fire."

Jimmy was mumbling excuses and explanations to me all over the place, but I told Jimmy, "It's not a catastrophe. It's just that it came out of the blue, and I should have told them. I'm not 16. I'll talk to them and explain what it's all about." When I got home I knew what the situation would be. My folks would be worried about my entry into racing. The only racing they were familiar with was the Indy 500. I painted as rosy a picture as possible about the difference between road racing and oval racing, that people just drove their cars to the track and raced them. Partly true. The conversation soon turned into laughing over Jimmy's reaction. My mom described it as "a little boy caught in the cookie jar."

The helmet story didn't quite end there. The following Sunday, Jimmy was up at the house and he asked me for a pen. "Does your mom have some clear nail polish?" I looked at him and he just said, "Come on, it's not for me, see if you can find some." I said I would take a look, and went into my mom's dressing room, something I never did. I found a bottle sitting on her make-up counter. Jimmy took the helmet and signed his name on its left hand side. Then he protected his autograph by putting a light covering of clear nail polish on it.

Jimmy said, "Now I'll always be in the car with you." I made light of it. I said something like, "You'll have to be the passenger." Being the passenger was always a standing joke with us, but later on in my racing career, when I had put Jimmy's old helmet on the shelf because it was no longer "state of the art" and I had a new one from England, I copied Jimmy's signature on the side of the helmet and protected it with clear nail polish. I wore that helmet throughout the rest of my road racing career.

We were now coming up to the end of August and the Labor Day road races. Jimmy, who pushed everything aside including *Giant*, had taken over the whole deal like an expectant father. He was going to oversee my pit crew, which consisted of two cousins, a stockbroker friend of mine, and the 15-year-old son of a friend. Jimmy wouldn't let anyone but himself accompany me through technical inspection. Tech inspection was where all cars were checked for seat belts and the way they were anchored, exhaust systems, brakes, and checked for any non-production additions to the car. No matter how many races you drove or won, tech inspection was about the car, not the driver, and every car was inspected before every race weekend. There was a

Jimmy & Me

Competition Committee that oversaw driver's performances or lack thereof, and dealt accordingly on infractions and dangerous or inept driving.

The plan was for me to drive up Friday morning and, because of *Giant*, Jimmy would be coming up Friday late afternoon. As it happened, just a few days before our Friday departure, I received a phone call from a young Warner contractee, Jeanne Baird. She must have got my number from Jimmy, because I didn't know her. Jeanne said she was a friend of Jimmy's, and she knew that Jimmy and I were going up to Santa Barbara for the races, that she would be in Montecito in a friend's beach house, and that Jimmy and I were welcome to stay there. I told her that would be great, and I would tell Jimmy. Jeanne said that Jimmy already knew and had left it up to me. I accepted quickly — a house on Montecito beach beats a motel every time.

I drove up as planned on Friday in my Porsche with my racing helmet on my head. I was really into this adventure. Jeanne was there when I arrived, and showed me the twin-bedded room that Jimmy and I would share. We spent the next couple of hours just sitting in the sun, with Jeanne asking about Jimmy's and my friendship, and about what we did. Everyone seemed to have a curiosity about our relationship. Jimmy showed up on schedule about 5:00 p.m. It was a very warm day and we got into our bathing suits and went down to the water. There was a raft anchored about 50 yards off the shore, and Jeanne and I immediately swam out to the raft and climbed aboard. Jimmy was standing at the water's edge, watching us, so we waved for him to come on and join us. Jimmy just stood on the shore smiling and answering our yells with the one finger salute. Yes — that's the one: the middle finger.

I have long since wondered why I never saw Jimmy go into the water. Not at our pool. Not at the beach. I'm sorry, but I can't tell you why. Could Jimmy swim? I think so; he was athletic. Was it because he wore glasses all the time? I just don't know. Jimmy never went in the ocean that weekend, even after coming back from the first day of the races — hot and gritty from the dust and fumes. When Jeanne and I again went swimming out to the raft, Jimmy just watched from the shore. I learned just recently, in conversation with my friend, Marcus Winslow, that Jimmy used to swim at the "old swimming hole" on the Winslow Farm. So much for that mystery!

When we hit the sack that first night, with Jeanne in one bedroom and Jimmy and me in the adjoining bedroom, the lights were out and the doors were open when Jimmy started to fool around on the "square," as we used to say, by starting a sing-song: "Oh Jeanne, where are you?" and "Say the word Jeanne, oh Jeanne." And Jeanne was answering in the same sing-song way: "Oh Jimmy, forget it!" and "No way José." I just laughed and finally we went to sleep.

Jimmy and I left for the Santa Barbara Airport in Goleta, the site of the races, early Saturday morning. We put the car through tech inspection, and with Jimmy mothering me through the entire process, we found our way to the pits and our car spot. I was excited and a little nervous, but I was destined to be nervous before all my races until the flag went down. Not fearful, just adrenalin. Of course Jimmy was the big attraction in the pits, but he kept telling people that he was just there for me — that this was my racing weekend, not his. No one had any idea who I was. I was a non-entity to them if ever there was one, except for the fact that Jimmy and I were obviously there together and Jimmy was my pit boss. That was one huge exception. The pit boss makes the final check on everything before the race: tire pressure, gas in the tank, windshield clean. And making sure the car starts. But there wasn't much to be done on a Porsche 1500 standard Speedster. Just drive it.

Jimmy & Me

Jimmy did do a lot of visiting in the pits. He loved being around the machinery and talking to drivers and mechanics. He loved the smell and the roar of the engines. I did too, but I was captivated by driving. I was always competitive in sports. I was an accomplished tennis player and had played basketball, like Jimmy, in high school, and I always wanted to win. My pit crew, in the meanwhile, would fool with the car. All they knew how to do was wash the windshield and go down to the gas truck and put gas in the tank.

There is a picture taken by Sandy Roth, just a snapshot, showing Jimmy and me visiting another Porsche driver, Dale Johnson. Dale, at that time, was one of the leading Speedster drivers. It shows Dale and Jimmy talking while I'm peering into the engine compartment. I have no idea what I was looking at, but we did a lot of that during the weekend — walking around the pits, talking to drivers and staring into engines. I didn't know Sandy Roth at that time, and I didn't even know he was up there shooting.

And then I drove. For the first time in my life, I took the car out on the starting grid to await the signal to get in, buckle up, and turn on the ignition. I was perhaps one or two lines from the end of the pack, being a new driver with no record. There were Porsches, TR3s, MGs of all types — and even a VW or two. I had no idea what was to come. I had gone around the track during the practice period so at least I knew how it was laid out, where the tight turns and the sweeping turns were, and the length of the straightaways, And where the "esses" were. And that's about all I knew.

All of a sudden the starter's flag went down and the entire starting grid moved as one. I moved with them like a steer in the middle of a cattle drive. It was a short run to the first turn, a right hander off the short front-straight into the "esses" — a series of immediate right-left turns. I was aware of driving while at the same time being in a kind of a fog. I was relying on instinct and instinct alone as I shifted both up and down to get through the "esses" and then a right hand turn to a straightaway. I think I was mainly concerned with not banging into anybody more than I was trying to pass other cars. For me, this was completely virgin territory.

I got through the "esses" and passed slower cars on the straight, which led to a sweeping right-hand turn onto the back straight — the longest straight at Santa Barbara. I felt more comfortable on this portion of the track, and was actually looking to pass other cars, but I was a long, long way from beginning to understand the art of sports car racing. I wasn't even thinking about how fast you can take different turns without spinning out; i.e. your "line" through the turn. Or how deep you can go into a turn before you hit your brakes and begin the process of shifting down in the gears.

These are the vital elements that separate drivers. Jimmy and I both were of the opinion that race driving was an art, not a sport. Like any other art, racing, especially sports car and Grand Prix race driving, was the individual gift the driver had of hand-to-eye coordination and depth perception that separated him from others. At that time, England had the #2 driver in the world, Stirling Moss, and Argentina had the #1 driver in the world, Juan Manuel Fangio. Both of these great drivers drove for the World Championship team of Mercedes-Benz. Fangio, whose driving style was very smooth and easy on the machinery, was faster per lap than Moss. It was that infinitesimal difference of Fangio's line through the turns, and an inch or two deeper into the turns before braking. That was the difference. Moss was more hell for leather then and sometimes didn't finish a race.

Jimmy & Me

I bring this up because Fangio was my idol and I was to pattern my whole approach to race driving on his style. I believe that my driving more closely resembled Juan Manuel Fangio while Jimmy's, in his short career, was more like Sir Stirling Moss. In the early races — and he only did three — Jimmy seemed to drive as fast as he could, sometimes faster than physics would allow. But just the three. We don't know how he would have evolved as a driver, or what influence my style would have had on him, if any. I drove in over 35 races and l lost count of practice laps. I didn't reach sports car racing stardom until I had raced about a dozen times.

My first race lasted eight laps. I have no idea if my lap times got any faster, or if I just beat the cars and drivers slower than I was. One thing I did learn, I could beat slower cars but only if they had average drivers. I was beaten soundly by at least one MGA driven by an excellent and experienced driver, E. Forbes Robinson from England. "Robby" and I were to become good friends, but for the first six months my goal was to come in ahead of him, and when I accomplished that, I felt I would have reached my first plateau — being able to beat a slower car driven by a top driver.

I finished my first race in the middle of the pack, which meant that I bested many of the slower cars driven by average drivers. I was not reasoning all this out that day. I was happy and excited that I had driven my first race without hitting a hay bale, or spinning out, or being hit by another car. My pit crew was all excited and so was Jimmy.

After the race Jimmy, my pit crew, and I stopped at the 101 Cafe, a very popular stop on Highway 101 before the freeways were built. And of course the whole conversation was about my first race and how great I did. I basked in the compliments, but I was already thinking of how much I had to learn.

Lew Bracker

I was completely confident that I could do this. I could be a winning driver.

That Saturday night, Jimmy and I invited Jeanne to have dinner with us, and we chose to go to what was generally considered the best restaurant in Santa Barbara, "The Talk of the Town". It turned out to be an interesting choice. Jimmy and I were dressed in khaki ducks, shirts, and light windbreakers because there was always a breeze coming off the ocean.

When we got to the restaurant, there was an argument going on at the entrance. It seems that a race journalist from England was there dressed in formal summer attire with a bow tie and jacket: the works, except for the short pants, which are considered formal in Britain and even worn by their military. Well, the Talk of the Town wasn't having any of that and would not let him in with short pants. Jimmy got a big kick out of this, as did we all because Jimmy and I were surely under-dressed compared to the gentleman in question. But our pants were long.

The Sunday race was different from Saturday. I was starting with only half as many cars in front of me and I had some knowledge and experience, not only of the track's turns, but of what goes on once the flag drops. And how to negotiate the race. After all, I had the experience of one full race behind me. It doesn't sound like much, but believe me, it made a big difference in what was going on in my head.

My driving on Sunday was, I am certain, more cohesive and faster per lap than on Saturday. I was conscious of looking for opportunities to pass other cars and having somewhat better lines through the turns, and going a little deeper into the upcoming turns before braking and shifting down.

Jimmy & Me

Everything was going well. I thought I had everything under control and as we approached the final turn of the final lap — a hairpin left turn off a short straight onto the main straight and the checkered flag — I had a TR3 in front of me who took the hairpin wide. I ducked under him by going deeper into the turn before braking and was passing him on the inside when he turned into my right rear fender. He simply wasn't a good driver, and when I passed him his reaction was to try to cut in from his wide line. All he accomplished was crumpling my fender but it didn't prevent me from finishing. I have seen a Sanford Roth photo of Jimmy's facial reaction to this collision. The tactic of going deeper into the turns—and taking another car on the inside — was to become a trademark of my driving.

Jimmy's biggest worry was my folks. We had spent a lot of time painting a picture of a "drive in the park" scenario, and here I was, taking my car back home with a badly crumpled rear fender. Later that afternoon, having coffee on the way back to L.A., we discussed this problem at great length and my plan seemed to be the best option. I wouldn't be getting home until after dark so I would pull into the carport in my usual place on the far right where the fender would be against the right wall of the carport. Being in the insurance business, having it repaired was not a problem. I would take the damaged car to the body shop the next morning, have it repaired, and no one would be the wiser. In retrospect, we were just like two siblings knowing they had crossed some line and were now conspiring to hide that deed from the parents. I carried out the plan, and my folks never were the wiser about the collision on the race track. Jimmy was relieved just because he didn't have to make himself scarce.

I had driven my very first race and gone through my first race weekend. Jimmy was by my side through that entire weekend and, while he loved being at the races, he was obviously anxious to get back into the action of racing himself. I was very aware that Jimmy was in his element at the races. Acting was his profession and racing was his recreational love. Both were art forms.

This was Jimmy's last weekend at a sports car racing event.

Chapter Fifteen

"AND THE DAYS GROW SHORT WHEN YOU REACH SEPTEMBER"

September's first weekend had passed. The big event of the month, as far as we were concerned, was behind us. And Jimmy was looking forward to finishing Giant, when his shackles would be removed. We were both looking forward to the future and our joint race events. We didn't know it, but Jimmy's Spyder purchase, and therefore the Salinas races, were only a couple of weeks away. Jimmy still had to finish *Giant*, and I had my job to do. But that didn't stop us from hanging out around town at night.

Jimmy and I were in great spirits. We were still on a high from the Labor Day Weekend. I had raced, and now we had even more in common. Jimmy would soon shed the burden of Jack Warner, Steve Trilling and, of course, George Stevens. We were now looking forward. It was all about the future, and all the races where both of us would drive. Jane Deacy was coming to town to negotiate and finalize a new powerful contract, and Jimmy would be making his own films for big bucks.

A new friend around Jimmy now — as far as I was aware— was Sanford "Sandy" Roth, the photographer on the *Giant* set. This seemed to be a pattern with Jimmy. He evidently respected really good photographers, perhaps because he liked photography himself. But it doesn't solve the mystery of Sandy being at the Santa Barbara races, but never around our pit, or where Jimmy and I were visiting. Yet, I have seen some photos of that weekend taken by Sandy Roth.

Lew Bracker

First Dennis Stock, and now Sandy Roth: Sandy was an excellent photographer and took most, if not all, of the stills of Jimmy on *Giant* that we have seen. Like Dennis, Sandy was aggressive in his personality, but Sandy was a talker, and he spoke with the confidence and authority of someone who had been everywhere and done everything. Dennis was kind of New York aggressive, but could be quiet and a listener. Sandy, it seemed to me, loved to hear himself talk — particularly about himself. Dennis never was like that.

I clearly remember the night Jimmy took me by the lower duplex in Hollywood that the Roths were renting. He merely said that he wanted me to meet someone. We were welcomed into the Roths with open arms. Sandy was clearly in charge with his rather domineering personality. I was to learn quickly that "domineering" was the right word to use to describe his relationship with Beulah, his wife. Beulah was a very nice and gracious woman, but completely under Sandy's thumb and, I thought, treated in a subservient manner. Sandy cut off her opinions or even contributions to the conversation on a regular basis.

I was very pleased to learn that after Sandy passed away, Beulah came into her own. She had command of all of Sandy's work, including his truly fine Dean pictures, and did very well financially with them. It was not only ironic, it was a tribute to the saying "What goes around comes around."

I was friendly with Sandy and Beulah even after Jimmy died. We had them up to the house for dinner one evening. Though I disliked the way Sandy treated Beulah, it was their business and they were always very nice to me. Sandy, as most know, was part of Jimmy's group on the way to Salinas. Sandy is the one who took the pictures of Jimmy and the Porsche Spyder at

Jimmy & Me

Competition Motors before they took off on that fateful trip, and took photos at the crash scene.

Jimmy started talking about having his own place at long last. Not something he rented, but something he would own – a house that would not only belong to him, but would also reflect something of who he was — something personal. It would be the first house he ever owned.

It so happened that I had a friend, Max Watkins, an insurance man specializing in estate planning. He owned a house in the Hollywood Hills and wanted to sell it and move his family to the Santa Barbara area. I had never seen the house, but I told Max about Jimmy and asked if I could look at the house and get a feeling of whether or not Jimmy would be at all interested. Max took me up to the house and, as I went through it, I knew that Jimmy might be really interested.

The house sat just below Mulholland Drive on the Hollywood side and not far off Laurel Canyon to the east. It had a fine view of West Los Angeles to the ocean on a clear day — of which there were plenty in those days. But the house itself was all Jimmy. It was a two-story, California-style stucco with red tile roof. When you came up the driveway, the house presented itself beautifully. But it was the inside that struck you. You entered into a foyer. On your right, with a two-step drop you were greeted by a pegged floored, huge-windowed living room with a beamed, vaulted ceiling. I knew that Jimmy would love this place even if you closed off the rest of the house. The house also had a lovely dining room, again with pegged wood floors. There was a large and light kitchen with pantry, bedrooms and baths upstairs, and a half-bath downstairs. I remember the asking price was $50,000.

Lew Bracker

I told Jimmy about the house and we went up there the next day. Jimmy was wowed, and was already telling Max and me his plans for hanging state-of-the-art long cone-type stereo speakers from the rafters. He was going to have a comfortable sitting arrangement that took advantage of the huge floor-to-ceiling windows on the south wall that looked out over West L.A. Jimmy was already talking like he was going to buy this house, and told Max that after his new contract was signed in October, he would do just that. Max was thrilled — not only because of selling the home privately and allowing him to move — but also because Jimmy was so in love with it. Max eventually did move to Montecito a few months after Jimmy died and prospered in one of California's most expensive and lovely communities.

It was later in September, the fateful day of the 18th, that I left work in the late afternoon. It was my practice to make my way north towards Hollywood to hook up with the Cahuenga Pass to Studio City and home. But in order to beat the boredom, I would take a different route almost every time. This particular day I decided to go up Rossmore, which would turn into Cahuenga and take me past Competition Motors. It was just something to do, but probably to see what was in the window. And what was in the window was a rare sight — a new Porsche Spyder.

When I got home I phoned Jimmy, really not thinking of anything other than to relay my bit of news because he would be interested. I didn't have any notion how interested. I said, "Guess what I saw today in Von Neumann's window? He has a new Spyder sitting there." Jimmy said, "Really?" He acted mildly surprised, but interested. "Yep, I just saw it," I answered.

Later, after Jimmy's death and thinking back about that conversation, I realized that suddenly he had wanted to get off the phone. He sort of cut the conversation short. I was vaguely aware of it because Jimmy never did that to me. I became

Jimmy & Me

conscious, looking back, that Jimmy knew immediately what he was going to do, and wanted to hurry and go do it. Jimmy was not going to tell me — he was going to show me. On the afternoon of September 21, just three days after that phone call, Jimmy drove up to the house in his new Spyder. I was surprised but not shocked. Certainly not shocked enough not to ask, "Where is your car? I want to buy it." Jimmy evidently hadn't given that possibility any thought. I wanted Jimmy's car — not because it was Jimmy's, like the situation would be in today's world — but because his Porsche was a Super and mine had a standard engine. This meant his ex-car was faster. Also, Jimmy had installed a special cross-over exhaust system, designed and made by Lance Reventlow's mechanic. This system eliminated a lot of the back pressure on the engine and the ensuing free-flow of the exhaust made the car more efficient, a little quicker, and a little louder. And it was legal under the production category rules in racing.

Jimmy said that his car was down at Competition Motors as he had traded it in. I immediately called them — of course I knew them well — and told them I wanted Jimmy's old Speedster. They held it for me. Not only did I buy Jimmy's car, I technically traded my car, which cost less than Jimmy's, even up. I was able to do this because I already had a buyer for them for my car. And that was how the deal was done the next day: Jimmy had his Spyder, I had Jimmy's Super, and my Speedster was in new hands, bought by a young couple from Minneapolis, Tod and Sue Dockstatter. Tod was a cartoon illustrator for UPA, the creators of the Mr. Magoo cartoons, but it was really Sue who wanted my beautiful red Porsche, with it's straw-coloured and straw weave-like interior. Everyone was excited about their new rides.

To give you an idea of the monies involved then when compared to today, here is a brief rundown: Jimmy paid $6,800 for his

Spyder, and got credit for $3,000.00 for his Speedster. I paid $2,900 for my 1500, and paid Competition $200.00 plus my car for Jimmy's car. My friend bought my 1500 from Competition for $3,000.00.

It was only two nights later, September 23, that Jimmy and I dropped in to the Villa Capri at about 7:30 p.m. to have dinner. This was rare because we almost never were there during the dinner hours. For some reason we were there at that time, and the place was full.

When you entered the Villa, you walked into the bar area where there was only one banquette — facing the doorway. It was a long table in front of a padded bench that curved at the end so someone could sit at the head of the table. It seated as many as eight and was open to the door and the bar. Nikko was very apologetic, and said that this banquette was the only thing he had available. Nikko had no problem with just the two of us sitting there, but he was very reluctant to put Jimmy out there as it were, instead of in a more private booth in the main dining room. We put Nikko at his ease, just wanting a table, so we were seated in the bar facing the door.

We were sipping our drinks. Mine was red wine and Jimmy had his usual wine/7-Up concoction. Jimmy wasn't looking around. At the critical moment, he was looking down — perhaps thinking. I always loved to people-watch, and so I kept looking as people walked in.

I was looking at the door when a couple walked in, looked at the packed restaurant, and left. I said, "Do you know who just looked in and left?" Jimmy asked, uninterestedly, "Who?" I replied, "Alec Guinness!" Jimmy jerked his head up. "Where?" "He took a look at the crowd and just left," I answered.

Jimmy & Me

Jimmy literally jumped up and ran out the door. He returned a minute or so later with Alec Guinness and his friend, who turned out to be the sister of producer Charles Schnee, Thelma Moss. Jimmy, who had never met Sir Alec, had obviously invited them to join us, and they accepted. Jimmy was really happy with this turn of events. An evening with Sir Alec was something Jimmy really wanted. I was just pleased to meet one of my favorite actors since his earliest films.

Alec Guinness was charming and interesting — you might even say captivating. Jimmy listened to him intently, and of course asked questions. After dinner when we were having coffee with our conversation, Jimmy did what he had been dying to do all evening. He took Sir Alec out to the parking lot to see his new Spyder.

They were back in a few minutes, and Alec Guinness was pale and shaken. I thought he had been taken ill, but that was not the case. Alec Guinness, upon seeing the Spyder, said he had an immediate vision of death — and he begged Jimmy not to drive that car. Alec later wrote about this in his autobiography. I was not present when this occurred out in the parking lot, but I was there when they came back in. Sir Alec related what had happened in no uncertain terms. He repeated in front of all of us, "Jimmy, do not drive this car."

Jimmy made light of it, even laughing it off. I must say, I didn't give it much thought either, dismissing it from my mind by the time I got home. Certainly neither one of us wanted to dwell on it, and we definitely didn't want to take it seriously. It was only afterward that I burned this incident into my memory bank. Alec Guinness delivered a dire warning that evening that was to go unheeded.

Lew Bracker

I didn't know it at the time, but Liz Taylor had given Jimmy a Siamese cat that he named "Marcus," either after his uncle Marcus Winslow or his cousin Markie — I didn't get the chance to find out. Jimmy, as with Cisco, wasn't looking for responsibilities other than those he already had. So he gave Marcus to Jeannette Miller, a starlet under contract to Paramount whom he had just started to date. That was Jimmy. Buy a race car and give away a pet in the same week — one is a responsibility while the other is a prized possession. I met Jeanette that same week.

I was really learning how Jimmy's mind worked, and his giving Jeanette the cat was — as far as I was concerned — Jimmy's way of saying goodbye. He was moving on. I know that there is an account of a purported interview where it was said Jimmy brought the cat over on the night before he left for Salinas. The problem is that other people have written or said that they were with Jimmy that same night. Jimmy must have been awfully busy that night.

We were now approaching the last week in September, and as one of my favorite songs goes, "… and the days grow short, as you reach September." Calendar-wise, the days do grow short as we go into September, but the song refers to an older man's wooing of a young woman and he sings, "And I haven't got time for the waiting game." Neither Jimmy nor I knew, or even had a glimmer of a thought, that the days were growing very short in September. And we didn't have time for anything.

Almost every conversation between Jimmy and me at this time was about the future: Jimmy's future contract and my joining him as producer; the planned restaurant; a Porsche/VW dealership, buying a house; marriage; raising a family; and road racing. These were the things we were talking about. Part of the mythology surrounding Jimmy is the "death wish" nonsense.

Jimmy & Me

Does this sound like someone obsessed with death? And I remind you, I was there — I was a participant — I didn't hear it from someone else!

Every subject, as we went into the final week of September, was about the future. I sincerely believe that at that point in his life, Jimmy was happier than he had ever been since his mother died. I am certain of it!

Chapter Sixteen

A WORLD OF HURT

Jimmy was in my ear almost every day after he bought the Spyder. He knew *Giant* would be finished and he would race at Salinas. "Come on, you know you're going," Jimmy would say and, "What's another football game, this is my first go with a Spyder." "It isn't just another football game, its USC/Texas and the opening game of the season and I've been waiting for this one," I consistently answered. "You've got plenty of company in the car." Sandy Roth, Rolf Wütherich (Competition Motors' chief mechanic who had come over from the Porsche factory), and at least one other friend — in this case Bill Hickman — were slated to go with Jimmy.

We had variations of this same conversation through September but they intensified, as we got closer to the end of the month. We weren't arguing — Jimmy was just trying to get me to make the trip. I love college football and I was really looking forward to this game. I had it all planned to go to the L.A. Coliseum right from the office for that Friday night game, September 30, 1955.

Jimmy would not let up. "You're going?" "Jimmy, you got this crowd with you. You don't need me." "Yeah," he said, "But they're — you know —just guys I know, and they don't really know what it's all about. They'll do their thing and drive the wagon." Oh, oh. Signals went up. "What do you mean by drive the wagon?" I asked right away. "You're towing the car, right?" "Yeah, yeah, but I want you to go so we can talk about everything as it's going on," Jimmy answered.

Jimmy & Me

I accepted this because it made sense to me, and I never considered Jimmy putting the Spyder on the highway, so I just said, "We will have a lot of race weekends coming up." And that was the truth. We were both anticipating all of the race weekends to come. Not competing against each other, because I would be racing in the Production Under 1500cc engine-size category, and Jimmy would be racing in the Modified group. He would be competing against the larger cars such as the Austin-Healey 100's, Jaguars, and the occasional Ferrari and Maserati. I, like my first race, would take on all the production cars like the MGA or any other MG model, TR-3s, other Porsches, Alfa Romeos and Morgans.

Modified cars were not thought of as street cars. You didn't drive them around town. Some, like the Spyder, were qualified by the DMV to drive on the street if they had bumpers, lights and a windshield. But these were cars where you had to drive by the tachometer, keeping the engine revs up so the engine didn't lug, and it was very difficult to do in town traffic. Driving on the open highway wasn't even thought of because, especially in the case of the Spyder, they were low to the ground. 1955 Detroit cars were high with long hoods, and you just couldn't see a vehicle you weren't even dreaming of. And the Spyder was silver – road-color — to boot, and would not only not have been seen on the road from over those tall hoods, but no driver would think to look that low on the road.

There is one question, the question above all, it seems, that people have asked me over the years. "If you had gone to Salinas with Jimmy, could you have or would you have tried to prevent Jimmy from taking the Spyder off the trailer?" I have asked myself that question many times, and I am certain of my answer. Jimmy would have listened to me where he would not have listened to anyone else who was in his party, and no one in his party would have objected to Jimmy putting the car on the road. I am also certain that even if Jimmy did not heed my wishes, he would have compromised. I probably could have prevailed to have him drive behind the wagon instead of ahead of it, because Jimmy would have wanted me in the passenger seat and that was the only way I would agree to that. And this is another certainty: all the time spent discussing the matter would have put Jimmy at the crossroads well after the other driver made his left turn off Highway 46.

That entire week saw Jimmy busy finishing his work on *Giant*, meeting with Jane Deacy, trying to get at least 500 miles on the Spyder before he raced it. And trying to get me to accompany him to Salinas. Finally, Friday, September 30, 1955 arrived and I didn't hear from Jimmy that morning and really didn't expect to. However, about 1:30 p.m. or so, I received a phone call in the office from Jimmy. I estimate the time because I didn't make a note of it, but I do know that I had returned from lunch and had been in the office for about 20–30 minutes.

"I'm at Competition Motors and we're about to take off. My dad is here to see us off too. Are you coming? It's your last chance?" I was surprised to hear that Jimmy's dad was there. He hadn't mentioned a word about his dad. Obviously Jimmy had made contact and invited Winton to see them off. I told Jimmy, "No, I'm all set. I'm going right from the office to the game, but good luck. Have a great ride but just try and learn how to handle the car this time out. It's going to be very different. I'll talk to you Monday." Jimmy then said the last words he would ever say to me: "Okay, but it's your funeral."

I left the office about 6:00 p.m. that evening with a lot of anticipation and excitement as I looked forward to one of my most pleasurable pastimes, and it still is — a USC football game. I didn't even give Jimmy and his Salinas trip a thought. I

Jimmy & Me

was in a great mood. Hot dogs, popcorn, soda and a football game — who could ask for anything more?

I experienced it all including SC beating Texas, and the world was my oyster as I left the Coliseum and drove up to Hollywood and the Villa Capri. Yes, I did occasionally go alone if Jimmy was on a date or out of town. I pulled in and parked and saw Sam Wise, a PR type who was paid by the Villa to plant the Villa name in the columns of the *Hollywood Reporter* and *Variety* dailies. He was having a smoke and getting some air, but when he saw me drive up in Jimmy's ex-car he blurted out, "Oh my God, I thought I was seeing a ghost." Being confused, I asked, "What?" "You haven't heard?" he asked. It was about 11:00 p.m. at night. "Heard what?" I was already going numb. Sam took me by the arm and said, "Let's go inside."

Sam guided me into the Villa, and by now I knew something bad had taken place, but my mind was blank beyond that thought. It simply was not going to anticipate anything. I remember that as I walked in, every face turned towards me. Patsy, Billy, Jean, Baron, Nikko — all stared at me. Patsy and Nikko came rushing over and just took me and put me in a bar chair. I think it was Patsy who said, "Get him a glass of wine." I definitely had retreated into numbness when I was told what I didn't want to be told. I felt nothing. Nikko said, "Jimmy was killed in a car crash in his race car." I knew that the races didn't begin until Saturday, but I couldn't grasp the fact that they were talking about a crash on the highway. No one went into any more detail, if they knew any more. They, particularly Patsy and Nikko, just wanted me to sip some wine and sit there.

I did sit there, but I wasn't fully accepting the information. There must be a mistake. It was too final. Death is so final. What about our plans?

Lew Bracker

I knew I had to call home. I had this sense of urgency that my folks didn't know for certain where I was, although if I had had the ability to think logically, they knew I would never have gone away for the weekend without telling them.

But all I could think of was calling them because I hadn't been in contact with them since breakfast. All I could think of was that I knew they would still have the fear that I was in the car with Jimmy.

Jean Leon handed me a nickel for the pay phone and I called home. I was really sleepwalking, or acting zombie-like, but I knew I had to let my parents know I was alive and well. This was a time before answering machines, and no one was home. I instinctively knew that they would be gathered at my sister's home, so I called there. My sister Midge answered. I said, "This is Lew." Midge said, "Hold on," and my dad got on the phone.

They had all gathered together because the news reports indicated that Jimmy had a passenger with dark curly hair (Rolf), unidentified as yet. My family, on the one hand, didn't think I would go off and not let them know. But on the other hand, they were starting to believe that I was the "dark, curly-haired" passenger.

I didn't want to talk. All I could think of was getting home. My dad asked, "Are you all right?" "I'm okay, I'm going home." "Do you want us to come and get you?" he asked. "No." "We'll see you there." Conversation over. I told all my friends at the Villa that I was going home, and they too were concerned about my getting home, and wanted me to let one of them drive me — but I just wanted to be alone. Get home, and be in my room. It was the only thought in my head.

Jimmy & Me

I cannot tell you how hard it is to translate that evening into words even after 57 years at this writing. Firstly, I was in a walking coma through most of it yet, somehow I remember that night as if it were last night. I thought I had buried it in a corner of my memory bank, a door not to be opened. I began to write this chapter and simply stopped cold when I came to the night of September 30. It was all so clear in my mind that I was reliving it all over. I sat down to continue writing a few times but kept putting it off, and with good reason. As I write the words in this chapter I find myself getting emotional and fighting back tears — are these the tears I didn't shed that night?

I wasn't prepared, if anyone is ever prepared for the tragic loss of someone very close. And for the first time in their life. I am revisiting, for the first time, everything that I felt or failed to feel that night. Yes, I was numb and in a daze, but I was functioning mechanically and I do not remember the drive home. My mind, for the most part, had shut down in a way psychiatrists would explain as a way to protect myself. I wasn't thinking, just driving like a homing pigeon. I drove by rote. I stopped at stop signals and drove under the speed limit. I drove. That's all I did.

When I got home there was little conversation. My mom gave me a sleeping pill, something I had never taken before, and told me, "Just go to bed." I felt like I had a big hole in my gut. I felt empty. I don't even know if I had accepted what had happened, that tragedy had entered my life. I wasn't thinking about any details — certainly I was in shock — certainly I was traumatized.

I changed into my pajamas and got into bed, a night like any other night, except my mind was empty. It was concentrating on every little chore that we all do mechanically: brushing my teeth, taking off clothes, putting on pajamas and turning off the light. I focused on every little chore. My bedroom door was closed and would remain so for the next 48 hours. My body and mind were exhausted and I slept with the aid of the pill.

The weekend was a blur. I never got out of my pajamas or my room, spending the time in a closed room with my music. I probably played music so I wouldn't think. Yet, I had purchased a recording of Lenny Rosenman's score from both *Eden* and *Rebel* and I was playing the *Eden* score over and over again. I seemed to find comfort in that score. Perhaps it reminded me of the beginning. I still have that LP and many years later, I took the recording to Lenny and showed it to him. He was quite touched.

The reader may think that I was being maudlin or wallowing in sorrow. But I believe, in retrospect, that I was doing myself good; that I had started the healing process. One of my maxims that I have passed on to my daughters is that self-pity is a luxury no one can afford.

Thankfully, no one came to see me that weekend. I know my folks had something to do with that. By Monday I was beginning to think. I phoned Nikko to ask him if we could go by his (Jimmy's) house so I could take personal things out of there before fans or thieves broke in. He readily agreed. An hour later found me dressed and at Nikko's. I found a cardboard box in the house and I put most every personal paper I could find on top of his desk. I didn't think of opening drawers or it felt too intrusive, probably the latter. I had no idea what I was going to do with these items. I just felt I had to take them.

When I was done, I took the box, said goodbye to Nikko and went home. The contents were in my possession for over forty years, and now they are at the James Dean Museum in Fairmount, Indiana.

Jimmy & Me

Monday afternoon, my friend Jack Gray; who was a part of my pit crew and who had spent the Santa Barbara races with Jimmy and me (and was to be an usher at my wedding), was my first visitor when he and his wife, Mary, drove up to the house. I met them at the front door, and as they came up the entrance steps they began crying. When they started crying, tears rolled down my cheeks for the first time. We threw our arms around each other. Jack and Mary spent a few hours with me and it was good. We reminisced a little and even laughed a little. We couldn't believe it, but we did believe it. How could all this be ended? It had ended. There was no wiggle room. There never is with death.

Tuesday, Dennis Stock came up to the house. Dennis was somber but business-like, and while sad, was not nearly as emotionally involved as I was, or at least he handled it better. After talking about what happened, Dennis said, "You're going to the funeral?" It was more of a statement than a question. And before I had time to answer, "We'll go together." I'm sure I looked perplexed. I hadn't even thought about the funeral, much less that I would be there. Dennis had been to Fairmount and knew the people. I hadn't and didn't. "I haven't even thought about going. I don't know anything about Fairmount," I finally said. Dennis said words to the effect that he would take care of the details. I said, "I don't know Marcus and Ortense and I doubt they know who I am." Dennis simply said, "You should be there."

Dennis called the next day to tell me that we had tickets and reservations for the Friday night, October 7 "red eye" on American Airlines to Indianapolis — that we would rent a car and drive to Fairmount in time for the funeral. I didn't care about going to the funeral. I didn't want to go anywhere. But Dennis picked me up and put me on the plane. He was not to be deterred.

I also received a phone call that Wednesday from Jane Deacy, whom I had never met. I didn't even realize she knew who I was. Jane introduced herself, although Jimmy had mentioned her a lot, and proceeded to apologize for asking me to come over to her suite at the Chateau Marmont on the following morning. That she would prefer to come to our house but she was up to her neck in details following Jimmy's death. I said I would certainly come to her, which I did. My impression of Jane was that of a very sharp and very able business woman, but who was visibly shaken by the recent events on a personal level. Not primarily from a financial standpoint. Jane hugged me and treated me like family.

It was a visit, not a meeting: it was during this visit that Jane told me about her recent talks with Jimmy: he had informed her about his wishes and instructed Jane to include me, specifically, in the Warner contract as producer of all Jimmy's films. She also told me how much Jimmy talked to her about me and my family and his comings and goings at the house. How much it meant to him. And then Jane told me something I was to cherish the rest of my life, and I am quoting her verbatim. "Jimmy and I had lunch a few days ago and he was talking about you. He said, "Jane, I have always wanted a brother — and now I have one."

I was to visit Jane Deacy a year later, as part of my trip to Fairmount and New York, and Jane could not have been nicer. She set up my hotel reservation and tickets to some Broadway shows, things she didn't have to do. I think she was doing them for Jimmy.

The first week in October was coming to an end. A large part of my life had come to an end and my outlook on life changed forever. I learned that everything in life is temporary — and we take for granted those that are most dear to us.

Chapter Seventeen

I NEVER SAID GOODBYE

The following Thursday, in the mid-afternoon, Dennis Stock came by the house, picked me up, and drove us to the airport.

Dennis, bless his soul, was handling everything — I was simply occupying space. I never had it in mind to go to the funeral. Or anywhere. Somehow on that flight the attendants (stewardesses in those days) seemed to sense — and I don't think Dennis said anything to them — what our mission was. That we were on our way to Jimmy's funeral. Why else would you take a "red-eye" to Indianapolis? The funeral was the biggest news in Indiana, if not the world. The attendants could not have been more solicitous and compassionate. They plied us with pillows and blankets, trying to make our flight more comfortable, and even offering us snacks without waiting for regular service.

I slept very little but Dennis seemed to do better. We landed at Indianapolis, rented a car, and followed the directions to the state highway that would take us to Fairmount. I did the driving on that trip — that was one thing I had proved I could do in my sleep. Or in my trauma.

Today, that drive takes about an hour, but it was 90 minutes in 1955. Our flight had landed at about 10:30 a.m., and by the time we were on our way, it was after 11:00 a.m. We arrived in the small town of Fairmount at about 1:00 p.m. for the 2:00 p.m. service and found the town was bloated with people who had come for the funeral. It wasn't a problem finding the Friends'

Church. Finding a main building in Fairmount is an easy thing to do.

The church held about 600 people, and when we arrived, it was filled to capacity with a crowd of over 1,000 people standing outside with more coming by the minute. A P.A. system had been set up for their benefit.

I wasn't about to deal with the problem and was ready to call it a day, but Dennis told me to wait while he went inside and found Marcus Winslow, which is what he did. How he got in is beyond me, but Dennis was a New Yorker, so this probably wasn't a problem for him.

About ten minutes later, Dennis came outside with Marcus and introduced us, and it was immediately evident that while I didn't know Marcus, he knew exactly who I was. He took command of me, and led us inside where we sat with the family. In 1955, there were a few family members besides Ortense and Marcus Winslow, and Jimmy's father Winton — Jimmy's maternal grandfather, John Wilson, and his paternal grandparents, the Charles Deans, were there.

I sat there waiting. Just waiting for the service to begin. I didn't converse with anyone nor did I think about anything. I was probably still in some state of shock — at least I didn't want to deal with the stark reality of Jimmy's death.

The service was conducted by Dr. James A. DeWeerd, who had known Jimmy since he came to Fairmount. Eventually it began after a delay caused by the immense crowd. Fairmount and the Friends' Church had never had to deal with so large an event.

I don't remember much about what Dr. DeWeerd said, but he made references about a fast life. I immediately took umbrage!

Jimmy & Me

What is this guy talking about? But it seemed to be the direction Dr. DeWeerd was going.

I was struck by the thought that all these people had come to say goodbye to Jimmy. I realized then, I had no intention of saying goodbye. I was willing to be in attendance while everyone said their goodbyes — yes, even to the gravesite — but I was not about to bury our friendship.

I have a firm belief that no one is gone, as long as someone remembers them. I knew I was going to remember Jimmy forever. But getting back to Dr. DeWeerd's eulogy and its theme: I immediately disagreed when he quoted a sonnet of Edna St. Vincent Millay's to make his point: "My candle burns at both ends. It will not last the night; But ah, my foes, and oh my friends, it gives a lovely light!"

A lovely sonnet it certainly is, but in my opinion, it had no correlation to Jimmy. Jimmy was not burning the candle at both ends any more than Marlon Brando, Ben Gazzara or any other young rising star of those years. In point of fact, Jimmy was settling into a more routine or organized way of life. With the prospects of a huge boost in income on the immediate horizon, Jimmy was getting more settled rather than what his critics liked to call his "wild life." Yes, people love to point to his supposed death wish and his speed craze that they read about, which to them was proved by his racing.

But they ignore the fact that Jimmy had given up his motorcycle, a more dangerous mode of transportation enjoyed by millions of people. And they gave a complete pass to the likes of Brando, Lee Marvin, Van Johnson, and quite a few other Hollywood personalities who were running all over the desert on their cycles. In fact, Van Johnson was critically injured in a motorcycle accident early in his MGM movie career.

Lew Bracker

In my opinion, all that "wild life" reference was more a case of an impression based on rumor and innuendo and fueled by the Hollywood media. The gossip columnists pursued their take on the James Dean they wanted to exist because it made great copy. Their agenda was that James Dean had a death wish, but somehow, Brando and Marvin were simply macho. They pointed to Jimmy's love of sports car racing and motorcycles, but in later years Paul Newman and Steve McQueen also raced. And Steve McQueen, who I knew personally, loved bikes and rode them all the time.

When I returned from Fairmount, I visited the local library. I wanted to read some of Millay's sonnets just to see if I could find something more appropriate that Dr. DeWeerd could have used in his sermon. I found a line that stayed with me all these years: "Childhood is the kingdom where nobody dies that matters." I found this compelling. I had never lost anyone close, and in that respect, I had been in the kingdom where nobody dies that matters, but I had now been forced out of it. I think that is called reality and we are all destined to meet up with it. To be forced out of the kingdom.

I am a fatalist. I don't live in my childhood kingdom anymore. I am not delusional, yet I believe and have felt that Jimmy is in my life. James Dean has totally affected my life and my thinking.

After the service in Fairmount, it was getting on to 5:00 p.m. and darkness, and the family and close friends retired to the Winslow farmhouse. Marcus asked about our plans, and Dennis told him we were flying back to Los Angeles in the morning, and that we planned to drive back to Indianapolis that night.

Jimmy & Me

Marcus would have none of it. He insisted that we go back to the house and stay overnight with his family. I later found out that he had a very important reason for this.

We drove to the farmhouse where I endured the usual funeral talk by just standing around. I did enjoy meeting Jimmy's grandparents, but I was not looking forward to another meeting with Jimmy's father. Strangely enough, I cannot remember speaking to Jimmy's father ever again. Did I block it out? I doubt it.

Wow! I said I wasn't looking forward to talking to Jimmy's dad again, and yet I haven't told you about the first time I met him. Dennis, who was thinking of anything he could to help me during this time, thought that before we left for the funeral, he should take me by Jimmy's dad's house near Santa Monica Airport. So I let him take me there. Dennis knocked on the door and Winton Dean answered. Dennis knew Winton because he had accompanied Jimmy one day when Jimmy went there.

Dennis introduced me by name. It was evident that Dennis had phoned in advance. Winton said, "Oh yes, you're the insurance man. Do you know when I will be getting the check?"

I don't remember what I mumbled, but I certainly remember turning around and walking back to the car. I have no idea what the ensuing conversation was between Dennis and Winton except that it was short. Dennis tried to explain Winton's behavior on the way home, but I wasn't listening and really didn't care. I hadn't wanted to go there in the first place.

I don't want to make Winton out to be a heavy in my story. I have come to realize that Winton had his own demons to deal with. I don't think he ever quite recovered from his wife's death — and now his son's life and death. I doubt Winton had a real idea of where and how I fit into Jimmy's life. On the other hand, Dennis must have told Winton something in advance of our visit, just judging from Dennis' ultimate embarrassment. Dennis would not have gone over there cold turkey, particularly if he were bringing someone else.

From my vantage point today, I understand that Winton was not a strong person — and you can couple that with my relative youth at the time. I think that Winton bent with the wind, and that was why he shipped Jimmy off to Indiana when his wife Mildred died. I believe this was the core problem between the father and the son, and something that Jimmy (up to that time) had never forgiven him for.

As I write these paragraphs, it suddenly occurs to me that this was the core problem between the son and the father in *Rebel Without a Cause*! The son was stronger than the father — and the son was anguished that his father was not a stand-up guy.

As I relive those days, Jimmy did seem to be reaching out, if tentatively, to his father. Jimmy had actually phoned his dad and invited him to meet him and the group at Competition Motors on September 30th, and see them off to Salinas. When Jimmy phoned me that day in a last ditch effort to get me to go with him to Salinas, and told me that his father was there, I was genuinely surprised. Perhaps Jimmy was beginning to understand that his father was what he was and not what Jimmy wanted him to be. But Winton was not a bad man, and he was his father.

I was too young and inexperienced at the time to realize that Jimmy's exposure to my family, and my relationship with my dad, might lead (and definitely did lead) to an important change in Jimmy's thinking. I know now that Jimmy's acute observance of my interactions and relationship with my father would simply

Jimmy & Me

have to have an important effect on Jimmy's thinking. I believe it brought to the surface his lifelong hunger for a father/son relationship of his own.

Thankfully, it wasn't too long before Marcus cornered me and Dennis, and asked, "Could we go for a ride and talk a little?" Of course we agreed. We left the gathering and got into the car we had rented at the airport. And with me driving, Marcus in the passenger seat, and Dennis in the rear seat, we started off. All Marcus wanted me to do was drive around the Indiana countryside and talk. There was no destination, only a purpose. Marcus said, "Just tell me about you and Jimmy in California, about the things you did and talked about." I wasn't at all prepared for this, as that was one place I had no intention of visiting at that early date. "You mean just some of the places we went?" I asked. Marcus said, "Whatever you feel you can talk about right now, I'd just like to know." I never asked Marcus the why of it — because I felt that he would derive whatever comfort he could from whatever I could tell him — and that this was his own private business.

As I write this story I think, "If only I had already written this narrative at that time and could have handed it to Marcus. How happy, or at least pleased, he would have been that night." It would have given Marcus the one thing he seemed to need at that time. Sadly, I was 57 years away from sitting down with my demons and examining my true feelings of those past 16 months — and finally removing them from my locked mental compartment for examination.

After a few hours of driving around, and relating to Marcus some surface memories, we returned to the house. There was no possibility I could have related to Marcus all that I have told you. I was mentally incapable of doing that even had I wanted to. Upon our return to the house, we found that all the friends had left, and only the family was still there. No one asked us where we had been, so they must have known. I didn't have anything to say to Jimmy's family outside of the usual attempt at comforting remarks. In truth, I said almost nothing. Dennis, who had met these people on his trip to Fairmount with Jimmy for the *Life Magazine* shoot in February of 1955, was much more talkative and reminisced about that trip. Finally, everyone went home and we all went to bed after a long and trying day.

I haven't said much about the burial service because, once again, I was just there. I don't remember the service at all, but I did have a private mission that I kept completely private — even from Dennis. Actually, I thought that we wouldn't even attend the service except for what I was really coming to Fairmount to do.

By way of explanation: When you enter a race and actually run the race, each driver is given what we call dash plaques. These are little metal plaques that carry the logo of the road race organization, as well as the date and place of the road race. They also give the driver a little key chain that carries the same information, commemorating the event.

Once I knew I was going to Fairmount, I planned to bring these mementos from Jimmy's three races, plus mine from Santa Barbara. When the gravesite ceremony was over, I hung back until I was the only one at the site. I buried these personal (and very much a part of Jimmy and me) items deep in the grave — so Jimmy would have them forever. It was between Jimmy and me. I didn't mention it then or ever since — not even to my daughters.

Dennis and I spent the night at the farmhouse, and we left the next morning in time to get back to Indianapolis and our flight to L.A. Before I left, and at Marcus and Ortense's request, I

Jimmy & Me

promised to return for an extended visit the following year. Marcus stated that he was going to get tickets for the Indianapolis 500 for himself, Markie, and me. So that pretty well locked in the date of my return visit, which had to include the Memorial Day weekend of 1956.

We returned to L.A., and I thought that for most, if not all, of the attendees, the funeral service and the gravesite ceremony put closure to the passing of James Dean. Was I wrong? Obviously, for me it did not — I never put closure on our friendship. I acknowledged that Jimmy was no longer a physical presence. But that did not mean, to me at least, that our friendship had to end. And I was not going to let it end — it wasn't an option.

Jimmy's life may have ended, but his legend had begun. An almost astounding outcry of mourning and remembrance burst forth from millions of fans all over the world. Literally, hundreds of fans drove to Fairmount on any given day, to visit Jimmy's gravesite. Many of those would actually knock on the front door of the farmhouse to try and meet the Winslows. Marcus and Ortense, being the wonderful people that they were, were very gracious with these unannounced and uninvited guests. To this day, the farm and the gravesite attract many visitors.

Jimmy's physical presence in my life had ended, but our friendship continues. And my relationship with Fairmount, Winston, Ortense, and Markie also continues. Markie is now Marcus Jr. He and I have visited and communicated throughout the years. Whenever I would say to Marcus that Jimmy and I are still great friends, he understands exactly what I am saying.

Chapter Eighteen

EPILOGUE

The first thing on my mind after I returned from Indiana was to visit Rolf Wütherich to see if there was anything I could do for him. I knew that Rolf could not speak English, and that he had been transferred from the hospital at Paso Robles, California, to the White Hospital in Glendale, just a few miles from Warner's studios.

I prevailed upon Jeanette Miller to contact Ursula for me, who spoke fluent German and could translate for Rolf. I didn't have Ursula's telephone number and I knew that both of them were on the Paramount lot. We set up a lunch date for the three of us at the Paramount studio commissary. I explained to Ursula what I wanted to do and asked her if she would come with me to see Rolf and act as my interpreter. Of course, Ursula agreed.

Actually, this also might have been a little show of independence on her part. She was now seeing John Derek, who had a reputation as a controlling person. As a matter of interest, while I was sitting in the commissary talking with Ursula and Jeanette, I spotted John Derek. That wasn't difficult because he made himself very visible standing in the aisle with his dark glasses on, just staring at us. Me in particular. Derek wanted Ursula to know he was keeping an eye on her.

Ursula and I made our trip to White Hospital; Rolf and Ursula had a conversation in German in which he assured us he was being well taken care of and there were no visa or legal problems. Rolf was really banged up. It was a wonder he

Jimmy & Me

survived the crash. Sadly, years later he was killed in an auto accident in Europe.

I took Ursula back to Paramount and never saw her again. Oh, yes, except for one memorable night about 15 years later in Jean Leon's La Scala Restaurant. Ursula was now an international star and was in town, presumably, talking business with two men sharing her booth. I came into the restaurant with my wife, Phyllis, and we were seated in a booth directly opposite Ursula's. Ursula was not looking at people; she was concentrating on her conversation. By that time Ursula was used to people looking at her and she knew how to avoid eye contact.

I sent a note over to her via our waiter which said: "Lew Bracker, remember me?" Ursula asked the waiter where I was sitting, and he pointed right across the small room. Ursula looked over, her eyes wide, saw me and gave me a big smile. She was sitting in the center of the booth, but she shooed one of the men out and came over. We engaged in a big hug, right there in the middle of La Scala, with Jean Leon beaming. For Ursula, Jean, and me, a lot of memories went into that hug.

When I returned to L.A. from Fairmount and the funeral, I came back to a different L.A. and to a changed life. I am speaking not only of the obvious changes that involved the absence of Jimmy in my life, but the unexpected changes — also because of Jimmy. I was besieged with interview requests from magazines, newspaper reporters and local TV programs. Overnight a James Dean phenomenon was sweeping the country, if not the world. I wasn't at all prepared. I hadn't thought about or anticipated anything like this. In my mind, after the funeral, everything pertaining to Jimmy would slowly fade away as far as the public was concerned. Certainly once all three of his films had run their course. Wrong! As we now know, the legend never died, and the films never quit being shown.

Lew Bracker

What I came to call the "James Dean thing" started the day after the funeral. And in the day or so it took to get back to L.A the momentum was building fast. A reluctant celebrity, I was much in demand to tell what I knew of Jimmy. My mind-set, which was adjusting to this new phase, was now telling me that a few weeks more and all this will be a memory. Yet some fifty years later I found myself filming an interview for the BBC, and another one for a German crew for a documentary on Jimmy that was shown on all the German-speaking stations in Europe.

No, the "James Dean thing" never faded. My initial reaction to all the requests was one of not wanting to do any interviews, much less TV appearances, but the photographer Dennis Stock asked me to do an interview with a friend of his from the *New York Herald Tribune*, Joe Hyams. Dennis explained that Joe was a straight-up guy who would not misquote me, and that this would be a good way for me to counter at least some of the nonsense about Jimmy that was already beginning to surface. I agreed to meet Joe, and I would then decide after that whether or not to do the interview. On that condition, Joe and I met the following Tuesday night at the Villa Capri. This was the third week of October.

I liked Joe. He was a reporter and a nationally syndicated columnist and noted magazine writer. As it turned out the interview we did was the first major article on Jimmy and a very fair one. It ran in *Redbook Magazine*. Joe and I became close friends — a friendship that lasted until his passing in 2009.

After the first interview, Joe went on to write two books about Jimmy. But even he succumbed to putting some rumors and a little fiction into his books. I chose to consider it poetic license.

Dennis Stock and I continued to do things together, but he finally gave up on a Hollywood career and moved back to New

Jimmy & Me

York, to continue as a highly regarded and highly paid photographer. Dennis also remained a good friend of Joe Hyams, who engineered a get together at his and Elke Sommer's house in December of 1991 that included Lenny Rosenman, Dennis, Jeanette Miller and Faye Nuell. Faye was a survivor of the *Rebel* cast and a friend of Jimmy's. You might call it a reunion of the cast of characters from *The Days of 1954-55*.

The Hyams/Sommer marriage was on the rocks at this time. I wasn't quite sure if they were separated or divorced because, in typical Hollywood fashion, they were still sharing the house, so Elke was not at the gathering; she was in Europe. Their house had a pool and a tennis court, and Joe and Elke were avid tennis players. I had played tennis most of my life, so I had been on their court many times. When my girls were younger, we often went to Joe's and Elke's house on Christmas Eve. Elke would play her guitar and sing traditional German Christmas songs. The gathering of Joe, Dennis, Jeannette, Faye (who was also Natalie's stand-in on *Rebel*) and me was the last time we were all together. It was also the last time I saw Dennis Stock.

I have always enjoyed cooking and — given my Nogales roots — Mexican food has long been a specialty of mine. So I cooked a big Mexican dinner for the group. My daughter Lesley joined us. It pleased me that at least one of my daughters (the other lives in England) was able to get a close-up sense of what things were like during the James Dean times.

Lenny Rosenman and I remained life-long friends and we saw each other whenever we could. Lenny, Joe and I would meet for lunch — as a trio or as a pair — from time to time. At one time Lenny was holding music seminars at his home once a week. Joe and I, and sometimes Lesley, would attend and one night we even brought Dick Clayton. Lenny went on to win two Academy Awards and many Emmys. His career in Hollywood spanned 46 years, which included a dozen or so movies and at least 14 TV series. Lenny passed away in March of 2008.

An actor once said "the trouble with getting old is that you begin to lose your cast of characters". Within one year I lost two of the most interesting characters I had ever known — friends for over 50 eventful years: Lenny and Joe.

Dick Clayton and I saw each other just a couple of times, but he was such a nice guy. He even did all he could to direct insurance business my way after Jimmy's death, and that included steering one of his young clients, Tab Hunter, my way. Jeanette Miller and I sort of went together for a while, but it was never serious, although Jeanette was well within my preconceived parameters. She was Jewish, very pretty, and she had a great figure. We did pal around, going up to the ranch and to movies. And one night we did what Jimmy and I once did: we drove out to Castle Rock, sat on the rock, listened to the surf and gazed at the star-filled sky — talking only when there was a comment that demanded to be made.

I saw someone from the *Rebel* days only one other night, and that by chance. I was at a now-defunct restaurant called Maple Drive with my daughters when Dennis Hopper walked in. We said our hellos, and he seemed pleased to see me. But my days on the Warner Brother's lot were over. That part of my life was a memory. I stored it away carefully.

The Villa Capri was to figure prominently in my life once again. I had asked on November of 1956 the future mother of my children — Phyllis Sallet — to marry me. She said she needed time to think about it. About two months later we were having dinner in the Villa Capri. In the middle of the meal she stopped eating, looked at me and said: "Yes". I looked at her. She said, "Do you know what I am talking about?" "Of course," I

Jimmy & Me

answered. Jean Leon happened to be waiting on our table so he was the first one I told. Soon the entire Villa "family", including Carmine from the kitchen, came over with wine and toasted our engagement. They also brought a glass for Jimmy, and placed it on the table, where he would have been sitting, slouched in a corner of the booth.

This sums up what the months were like following September 30, 1955. And as the spring of 1956 approached I was involved in sports car racing and race cars. In December of 1955, just over two months after Jimmy died, I entered the Palm Springs races wearing Jimmy's helmet and driving his former car, the white Porsche Speedster. I won my first ever trophy by taking a second place. I should have been elated, but driving back to L.A. I was aware of emptiness. Jimmy wasn't around to talk about and to celebrate my trophy. We would not be laughing and toasting success at the Villa that night.

I was looking forward to my May trip to Fairmount that had been planned when I was at Jimmy's funeral. I had just purchased a newly configured Porsche 1600 Speedster, which had a 100cc's larger engine than the previous Porsches. Now 100cc's doesn't sound like much of an enlargement, but when you understand how small the Porsche engine was, that extra size becomes very significant. I have always loved driving, and like Jimmy, having bought a new machine I wanted to get it out on the open road. The prospect of driving to Indiana excited me. I was going to get my kicks on Route 66. And startle the natives in the bargain.

My trip was timed to get me to Fairmount on a leisurely schedule by May 29th. I began it by waving goodbye to my folks and heading eastward. It didn't bother me that I would have no radio — just driving the Porsche across the country was all that mattered. My plan was to connect with Route 66 somewhere around San Bernardino. Remember, there were no Interstate Freeways then. I wanted to avoid going through Hollywood, downtown L.A., Pomona and Riverside so I went the back way — across the valley through Pear Blossom and hooked up with 66 just north of San Bernardino. That route also gave me more hills and winding roads to enjoy.

I drove all that day straight through to Williams, Arizona. I remember picking out a local steak house, checked into a motel, had dinner and sent a post card home. The next day, after an early breakfast, I continued my journey with my next planned overnight being Amarillo, Texas. I arrived there in the late afternoon. I particularly remember the open-mouthed stares I was gathering, or more accurately, the Porsche was gathering. It was as if I were in a space ship.

The next day saw me driving through Oklahoma City headed for Tulsa. In those days you didn't by-pass any town — big or small — but I was delayed about 20 minutes between Oklahoma's two largest cities by construction of the future. The first freeway in that part of the country — I-40 — was underway. I had seen some of it being built as I was leaving L.A.

My trip continued through Springfield to St. Louis. St. Louis was my last overnight stop before Fairmount and I had been on the road across country with my ragtop down. So I checked into the Statler Hotel, found the barber shop and treated myself to a shampoo, haircut, shave and manicure. The bill was under $10.00.

That night, with nothing to do I did the usual — I looked in the movie section of the *Dispatch* and saw that John Ford's new film, *The Searchers*, had opened at a movie palace down the street from the hotel. Being a big admirer of John Ford's — and the film being Natalie Wood's next film after *Rebel* — I had no

Jimmy & Me

problem deciding what to do with my evening. When the Warner Logo flashed on the screen a pang hit my heart. I was suddenly transported back a mere eight months when everything was a lifetime of difference.

I took off early the next morning getting anxious to get to Fairmount. I didn't realize how much I was looking forward to revisiting the farm and the Winslows. A real visit this time. From L.A. to St. Louis it was simply an enjoyable cross-country cruise, but now the real reason for the trip took over my consciousness. Another thing that hadn't yet entered my head, but was soon made evident, was that the Winslows were looking forward to my visit with as much anticipation as I was. It was a lovely May morning and I had been blessed with great weather the entire journey. I hadn't even needed to put the plastic "windows" in place. And now, on my last leg, I had the sun in my face and the wind in my hair as I continued my pilgrimage.

Indianapolis was about 250 miles and about six hours away in those days, and you had to account for 30 minutes to drive through city traffic, with Fairmount another hour and forty-five minutes beyond that. I had it timed to arrive at the farm in mid-afternoon. Which I did. When I pulled into the farmyard and up to the house Marcus, Ortense and Markie were all there to greet me.

My visit to the Winslow farm could best be described as a bittersweet experience. Jimmy's gravesite was just down the road, and you had to pass it every time you went into town. This was a great deal different than being 2000 miles away. The Winslows treated me as one of their family. We talked. Marcus walked me around the farm and drove me around the country in his pickup. He showed me everything, explaining where Jimmy used to do this or that. He showed me the swimming hole that Jimmy used to play in, and his high school in Fairmount, now a closed relic. Decades later, Marcus Jr. also drove me around Fairmount. And much of Indiana.

I took Markie around in my Porsche, and of course it was the first Porsche ever to be seen in Fairmount — and most likely Indiana. One day Markie and I drove ten miles to the "big" city of Marion for an ice cream cone, and on another occasion, Jane — a cute high-school teenager who helped Ortense in the house — drove with me in the Porsche around Fairmount. Jane told me fifty years later that her boyfriend, whom she later married, was beside himself. She had to keep him from coming over to the farm to confront me.

On Memorial Day morning, Marcus, two local friends of his, Markie, and I set off for Indianapolis and the 500-mile classic. I remember the day vividly and so does Markie, now Marcus. We sat on the first turn, so we were able to see the cars coming down the front straight, into and around the turn, and into the back straight. It was a great day that we all enjoyed to the fullest, and discussed the race all the way back to Fairmount. Markie kept asking me questions, assuming that I knew all about driving at Indy, and in Offenhauser-powered cars. In the eight months since Jimmy's death I had been building a reputation as a sports car race driver of note, particularly as a Porsche pilot. That, however, was a different world from Indy-type racing and open-wheeled racing cars. I was able to explain a few things but honestly, racing where the cars just went in circles did not interest me. And I have never been to another oval-track race event since that day in 1956.

My visit to Fairmount with the Winslows was in two parts. I spent a week with them and then I left my car in their garage and took the train to New York to visit relatives. And Jane Deacy. I returned a week later. Marcus had been gracious enough to drive me to Marion and pick me up, necessarily to deal with the trains. I spent another few days with the Winslows before heading back to California.

My final days in Fairmount upon my return from New York City were spent driving around the countryside in my Porsche with Markie. Neither Ortense or Marcus ever got in the car. So we walked and talked and just sat in the house conversing. Marcus did take me around to meet townspeople. We had pleasant talks at mealtimes, and the conversations were mostly about everyday things. Actually, we talked very little about Jimmy. I think my being there was enough for all of us. Of course, we did talk about Jimmy's life in Fairmount, because Marcus was pointing out all the different places Jimmy frequented.

Before I left to go back to California, I was concerned that my new car would need an oil change, and of course there were no Porsche dealers. Not even in Indianapolis. I wanted to use Valvoline because that was the oil that Porsche dealers in L.A. were using, but where to find it? Marcus suggested I go down the road to the motorcycle shop Jimmy had used and see if they had any. So Markie and I took the Porsche down to the shop. Lo and behold — they used Valvoline for their bikes. I bought the required number of cans, borrowed a car jack and changed the oil. I have often thought how big a kick Jimmy would have gotten out of my changing my Porsche's oil in his old bike shop. To this day I am certain that my Porsche was not only the first, but perhaps the only Porsche ever to have been serviced in Fairmount.

The day finally came when I had to say my goodbyes to the Winslows, but I promised to come back. The Winslows, in return, promised to come out to L.A. sometime in the future. As it happened, I did return a few times, but Ortense and Marcus were gone by then and Markie had grown into Marcus. Marcus, Ortense and Markie did come to California and stayed at the legendary Hollywood Roosevelt Hotel on Hollywood Boulevard, across the street from the famous Grauman's Chinese Theater, and we had lunch there.

A few years later, after I had taken on a little more maturity, I began to feel guilty, or at least regretful that I didn't spend enough time with the Winslows while they were in town. I felt that I should have been with them more — and I still feel that way today. Was it because I never saw Marcus and Ortense again? The certainty is that I miss them.

As I come to the end of my narrative, my mind is filled with many freshly churned-up thoughts. I have revisited memories that were tucked away for a long time. And now, having pulled them out of their resting place and examined them, I find that I view them retrospectively — both people and events — much differently than I did at the time. After all I have much more of life's experiences through which to view those times. With experience, one hopes, comes wisdom and insight. At least much more than I had to call on at age 26.

I am thinking in particular of Nick Adams. I'm not sure why I am dwelling on Nick, but I think it's because of his inner conflict. And because, during the time of *Rebel*, I was the focus of his anger and jealousy. I didn't have the insight at that time to understand what was eating Nick, and why I was the chosen target for his animosity. I simply assumed that my friendship with Jimmy was at the base of it, and that Nick wanted to be that friend instead of me. From the perspective I have today, I have a better understanding of the conflicts and anger going on inside Nick. And I wish I could talk with him. One thing I would say: "I'm sorry. I'm sorry that I was not able then, mentally and emotionally, to understand and be helpful".

Jimmy & Me

I also have a much better understanding of everything I experienced with Jimmy — his friendship with Lenny and Dennis, and the problems that ensued in those relationships. But most of all, I have a better understanding of the Jimmy I knew. And I am now aware of all the lessons of life I learned through the Jimmy Dean experience. If they are still alive as I write this, there will be more than a few people who would tell me they knew a different Jimmy Dean. A Jimmy Dean with a dark side. And I would tell them that they may be correct — for themselves.

However, I would have to point out to them that they never saw the Jimmy Dean I saw in the summer of 1955. It is impossible to argue with anyone about their inner experiences. All I know is I never met the Jimmy they say they knew. I only knew the Jimmy I knew. Is their claim to their Jimmy as "real" as my claim to mine? I cannot say. I don't know what they experienced or what their expectations were. I simply had no recognition of the Jimmy they claimed to have known or been told about.

As I have said there are now more than 200 books about James Dean. Not one of those authors ever spoke to me with the exception of Joe Hyams, Porsche historian Lee Raskin, and author and teacher Pamela Des Barres. Most of these books have some of the same things in them, from practical facts and dates to repetitive rumors and myths treated as fact. Raskin's histories are the exception. Obviously, there is truth in all of them, but there is also misinformation and plenty of spicy speculation, except in Raskin's.

Do I miss Jimmy? I can only say that I am sitting here right now with my eyes welling up. I sit here thinking that maybe I have always told myself that our friendship is ongoing so that I wouldn't have to face my personal loss. I could think only of the loss felt by fans, by movie lovers, and thus keep a distance between me and my deepest feelings. I could answer questions and discuss Jimmy in terms of telling little stories and anecdotes without opening up that forbidden box that held my personal feelings.

I even held to this path with my daughters, whom I love dearly. I didn't realize, or didn't want to realize, how much they yearned to know everything, and how unsatisfying my ration of anecdotes must have been for them.

I thought I was handling it properly and that it was working well. Until I started writing this book. Now as the book draws to a close I find that I have at last opened that box and allowed myself to relive, without reservation, the whole experience. With this truly first examination, I feel a newly heavy heart and a fresh loss.

I also feel that my self examination is a good thing. It is long past the time for me to connect with my true self and my aching sense of loss. Time on its own does not heal wounds; it scars them over and reminds you where they are and the pain that you want to ignore. In writing this book I have learned something of great importance; I learned that you have to face your loss and your pain and be honest with it. Truly experience it and allow it to hurt. Then the healing can begin. Then you can truly embrace the memories rather than tuck them behind anecdotes and glib stories. I had not healed; I merely hid.

Please, Reader, I am not feeling down! I realize now that one deep feeling I have, and have always had, is the gratitude that, because of things happening in the way they had to happen, they happened to put my friend Jimmy in my life. The "chance" of certain people knowing certain other people, the circumstances and the timing that resulted in this meeting and that one — all of this for me meant a developing and rewarding friendship of 16 months. The most enjoyable, interesting and exciting period of my life.

I wish everyone could enjoy the experience of having a best friend, amigo, compadre or however you choose to describe it, who seemed to feel he was getting more than he was giving, and kept trying to give more in return. Where was this "loner," "taker," "rude and crude," "cold" James Dean? I don't know because I never met him. In my experience, it was just a great friendship ... Jimmy and me.

Things happen because they are meant to — and they happen at the exact moment that they do happen to make possible the event in question taking place at all.

About the Author

Lew Bracker was born in Nogales, Arizona and grew up in Los Angeles, California. He is divorced and has two daughters, one living in England and the other in Santa Monica, California. He now resides in Palm Springs, California. He is a U.S. Army Korean War Vet.

About Fulcorte Press

Fulcorte Press is devoted to bringing into digital format (and print-on-demand softcover) important books from the automotive world. Some of these books are great ones from the past – maybe now forgotten on dusty shelves. Their new life as easily portable digital books will find new readers and delight their old ones. Many of our books will be new to any form of publishing. We are all about rediscovery and discovery. Our website, fulcortepress.com, will carry information about not only our books and authors but reviews of other car books. Use it as an organized pathway to car books on the internet. And please inform us of books you know of that deserve a new format in life. Or maybe that book you've got inside clamoring to see print, whether real or virtual. We do both.

Printed in Poland
by Amazon Fulfillment
Poland Sp. z o.o., Wrocław